UNST

A few years after the turn of a new century, Wright was charging through a period of almost superhuman creativity, performing miracles of design and fresh sight, perfecting the Prairie Style even as he was leaping to other styles. He was bringing in commissions from the wealthy, living high, evading his creditors, cutting a handsome and rakish figure about Oak Park and Chicago. Neighbors watched him roar past in the "Yellow Devil," his custom-built yellow sports car, wearing aviator's goggles, and a leather helmet, sometimes with women other than Catherine Wright. He seemed unbeatable. Nothing could bring him down.

Nothing but the ingenious, intricate, demon-haunted, overburdened, and overworked genius mind of Frank Lloyd Wright.

READ ALL THE BOOKS IN THE
UP*close* SERIES

FRANK LLOYD WRIGHT

a twentieth-century life by
JAN ADKINS

PUFFIN BOOKS

PUFFIN BOOKS

Published by the Penguin Group

Penguin Young Readers Group, 345 Hudson Street, New York, New York 10014, U.S.A.

Penguin Group (Canada), 90 Eglinton Avenue East, Suite 700, Toronto, Ontario, Canada M4P 2Y3
(a division of Pearson Penguin Canada Inc.)

Penguin Books Ltd, 80 Strand, London WC2R 0RL, England

Penguin Ireland, 25 St Stephen's Green, Dublin 2, Ireland (a division of Penguin Books Ltd)

Penguin Group (Australia), 250 Camberwell Road, Camberwell, Victoria 3124, Australia
(a division of Pearson Australia Group Pty Ltd)

Penguin Books India Pvt Ltd, 11 Community Centre, Panchsheel Park, New Delhi - 110 017, India

Penguin Group (NZ), 67 Apollo Drive, Rosedale, North Shore 0632, New Zealand
(a division of Pearson New Zealand Ltd)

Penguin Books (South Africa) (Pty) Ltd, 24 Sturdee Avenue,
Rosebank, Johannesburg 2196, South Africa

Registered Offices: Penguin Books Ltd, 80 Strand, London WC2R 0RL, England

First published in the United States of America by Viking,
a division of Penguin Young Readers Group, 2007
Published by Puffin Books, a division of Penguin Young Readers Group, 2008

1 3 5 7 9 10 8 6 4 2

Copyright © Jan Adkins, 2007
All rights reserved
LIBRARY OF CONGRESS CATALOGING-IN-PUBLICATION DATA IS AVAILABLE

Puffin Books ISBN 978-0-14-241244-2

Printed in the United States of America
Set in Goudy
Book design by Jim Hoover

For

Maxwell Ulysses Burger, the Wild Thing

David Robertson Keller, the Pirate

Hannah Rose Kingsbury, the Peanut

CONTENTS

FOREWORD

FORTY YEARS AGO, I studied architecture at Ohio State University. I wanted to design real things for real people, to raise great walls and span them with broad roofs.

I had three great professors: Wayland W. Bowser, George Tilley, and Perry Borchers. All three were brilliant, but in very different ways. I didn't know it then, but they reflected three separate views of architecture.

Bowser beguiled us into believing that design was more than just pretty; it came out of human needs. He taught us that great design could make life better.

Tilley was a stickler for form and the professional etiquette of the drafting room. He stressed the unbending, physical reality of structure, the consequences of our work.

Borchers, an architectural historian, was abstract, acutely observant, distantly formal. He taught us that design was a process that began before us and would continue after we were gone.

Frank Lloyd Wright didn't fit into their architecture. I read his *Autobiography*, loved his designs, mouthed his phrases about organic architecture. But my intelligent and worldly teachers never mentioned him. He was a puzzling phantom. When I brought up Wright and the "organic" principles that excited me, they smiled faintly and changed the subject. They couldn't exactly ignore him, but they couldn't praise him, either. He was outside their world. They held their own three special views of architecture, and Wright had nothing to do with any of them.

He was, for architecture, what a black hole is for physics: an anomaly—something big and powerful that defies normal understanding. He was beyond Tilley's responsible rules, playing fast and loose with his own outrageous rules, but making them work. Wright went beyond Bowser's principles of design and even beyond his clients' needs.

He stood outside Borcher's history and flow of architecture. His best works sidestep time; they don't age, don't attach themselves to any era. Wright seemed to spring out of nowhere like a magician's trick, reinventing the entire profession of architecture for himself. In that sense, no one came before him.

And no one followed him. His students didn't become new Wrights. Wright's art was Wright. It couldn't be taught or transmitted.

I discovered that his long, varied, improbable life grew directly out of the world he knew, so that finding the person behind his art has been like reading a history of the twentieth century. I learned to love Wright all over again.

I'm grateful to him for the beauty and ingenuity he's created. I'm also grateful that the sly fox gave me a chance to revisit my dear professors. I've learned from Frank Lloyd Wright. Some lessons are positive: Look at these wonderful examples of creation! Some are negative: Don't ever get into this situation! As strange, annoying, complex, and colorful as the old rogue is, I hope you will enjoy him as much as I have.

INTRODUCTION

FRANK LLOYD WRIGHT was raised on his family's farm in the rolling hills of Wisconsin. He wandered across the country and across the world all his life but always returned to those hills. When he died he was buried there. Years later he was still wandering: his ashes were stolen and taken to the Arizona desert.

Life, any person's life, is strange in its particulars. Some lives have a plain shape like a long hill: they rise up slowly, reach a peak, and decline softly to their end. Some lives are short and hard, like the narrow walls of a quarry. Frank Lloyd Wright's life was like a mountain ridge in the Rockies: shooting up slopes and falling into canyons, up and down through rocks and forests, high and low, sunny and deeply dark. A wild ride.

His life was stranger and more curious than most for many reasons.

One reason is that it lasted so long, ninety-three years. He was born shortly after the Civil War and lived most of a century, to see early computers, airliners, atomic energy, satellites, and rockets preparing to reach the moon—the most radical changes in human history. His bright, extravagant life wound its way through half a dozen wars, major natural catastrophes, astonishing discoveries, international financial collapses, scientific upheavals. Throughout that lifetime, he was part of basic changes in the way people saw themselves and their lives.

Another reason his life was not ordinary was that Frank Lloyd Wright lived on the edge of disaster. He was a trouble-hound; he couldn't live simply or sensibly or even legally. He was always in trouble, always deeply in debt.

There were dark complications in his long life. Again and again it was battered by death and madness.

One of the simplest reasons for the strangeness of his life was that he was an extremely annoying man.

He was fussy, vain, and loud-mouthed. He was certain that he was a genius, smart, handsome, and something near a saint. He was eager to tell anyone, *everyone* about his glorious self.

But it would be foolish to stumble over little complications. The most important reason Frank Lloyd Wright's life was so strange is that he was a colossal personality. He was a genius, the most talented, original, and inventive architect our country—perhaps any country—has ever produced. Some architects have designed more buildings. Some have designed buildings that were more sensible and more useful. Some have been richer or have won more awards. But Frank Lloyd Wright was far and away the champion creator, the most imaginative artist with walls and roofs and windows and doors anyone has ever seen. When architects and historians are asked, "Who was the greatest architect of the last century?" they admit, sometimes reluctantly, that it was Wright. Many of them add, "And probably of the century before that, too." This one man changed architecture. He changed the homes we live in and the way we think about living. There is no doubt that he changed the way you live.

People loved Frank Lloyd Wright and hated him, often at the same time.

He was a rogue. This is an old word with several meanings.

One kind of rogue is a liar and a scoundrel. Wright lied. A lot. He lied about little things and big things—designs, expenses, schedules, ideas, friends, family. He tricked his clients and hid important things from them. He told them a house would cost $10,000 when he knew it would cost more than $100,000. He claimed to have all the drawings of a building when he hadn't even begun. He ignored his clients' ideas, wouldn't answer their letters and calls, and disappeared for months at a time. Then he borrowed money from them.

The thin difference between Wright and an outright swindler was that he didn't cheat people to get rich. He cared about only one thing: architecture. Clients and laws and money weren't important. The work was everything. He used clients and their money to create his architecture, whether they liked it or not. Somehow he swept his clients up into a kind of enchantment. They became hypnotized by his magical talk and fanciful promises. Under his spell, they wrote more checks and put up with his insults and eccentricities.

At times his clients realized that what Wright was building didn't have much to do with them or their lives. Some complained and demanded sensible limits. Wright ignored them. But when the building was finished (always late, always over budget) his clients wandered into their Wright homes in some kind of rapture. He allowed them to live inside his work of art. Most of them were grateful.

Another kind of rogue is a wandering beggar. Throughout Frank Lloyd Wright's long life he was always in debt. He bought groceries, hired carpenters and servants, bought fancy cars, had expensive suits made, and didn't pay for years, sometimes never. Sheriffs appeared with writs and warrants but he enchanted them somehow, and they went back to the jail without him. His bank account always insisted that he was poor, yet he traveled the world like a glittering prince.

The best kind of rogue is a tale-spinner, a mischievous troublemaker, a trickster. You know this kind of rogue: a sweet bad boy. You want to hit him on the head with a brick but you love him. Behind his impish smile and his wild behavior, Frank Lloyd Wright was always chuckling to himself, as if to say: How can I do something even more shocking?

Which rogue was the real Frank Lloyd Wright? All of them.

Would you have liked him? Maybe or maybe not, but he was fascinating. People wanted to be near him, even when they were angry at him. He was like a stage magician: you know that he's a fake but you love his illusions and you can't deny his skill.

Like him or not, he changed your life.

• 1 •

DARKNE$$ AND LIGHT

FRANK LLOYD WRIGHT wrote *An Autobiography* in 1932. A better title might have been *An Invention*. He disregarded the facts and reinvented his own life as a kind of fable to explain how he became so great— though at the time he had very few projects and was deeply in debt. In this fable about himself he rearranged events as he thought they *should* have been.

In *An Autobiography* he tells us he was born on June 8, 1869. But the birth records of Richland Center, Wisconsin, show he was born June 8, 1867.

Wright gives us the wrong ages for his mother and father, mistakes his father's full name, and even lies about his own name. Why lie?

Perhaps telling the absolute truth got in the way of his storyteller's flourishes. Or perhaps he enjoyed fooling people: he took a sly delight in twisting facts.

His mother, Anna Lloyd Jones, was usually called Hannah. She was a tall, broad-shouldered woman with a plain face. Anna and her five brothers and four sisters were part of the sturdy Lloyd Jones clan. The family had come from Wales to settle and farm a Wisconsin valley with rich soil and hard winters. Like her sisters, she was a teacher.

When she was twenty-seven, close to an age when some might call her an "old maid," she married William Carey Wright. He was forty-one. William was raising two young sons and an infant daughter after his first wife died. He was a handsome, gentle man with a powerful mind and extraordinary gifts. He taught, read poetry, sang, composed music, and played Bach, Brahms, and Beethoven on several instruments. He was a lawyer and a preacher known for his oratory, the art of making speeches.

Anna and William's first child together was given the name Frank Lincoln Wright. "Lincoln" was a popular name in the United States in 1867: both the Wrights and the Lloyd Joneses were northern anti-slavery families, and President Lincoln, the "Great

Frank in 1874, age seven.

Emancipator" who freed the slaves, had been dead only two years.

The couple had two more children together, Jane and Margaret Ellen, but by the time Meg-Ellen arrived, the Wright household had become dark and angry.

Wright's boyhood, like the rest of his life, was checkered with patches of darkness and light, depression and happiness. What happened to his family? The twisted tales in his autobiography say one thing. The facts from records and other witnesses tell a different story. Between the two stories, we can see how upset and confused young Frank must have been.

Some family stress came from moving. William Wright shifted from place to place when he took new jobs as a music teacher or a minister in Baptist churches. Naturally, his family went with him—they went off to Iowa, Rhode Island, Massachusetts, then back to Madison, Wisconsin.

Some stress came from poverty. William was charming, intelligent, and artistic, but he couldn't make much money. The United States was having a bad time after the Civil War; wages were low, money was tight. Preachers—even fine orators like William— were "genteel poor" who often lived on the charity of their church members. In 1878 the family returned to Madison, near Anna's brothers and sisters in Spring Green. Relatives gave the family some welcome support. Anna's brother James, concerned about the children, made a forty-mile wagon trip with a milk cow tethered to his tailgate so that they could have fresh milk every day.

These stresses might have been soothed, but not by Anna Wright. She had an uneasy mind and a furious temper. At first she was kind and motherly to her stepchildren but in only a few years she changed. She began to beat William's children by his first wife and terrify them. Their aunts and grandparents were afraid she would harm them seriously. The Wright relatives took in all three of William Wright's older children, in family homes away from Anna. William wrote to them and saw them whenever he could. Anna was glad they were gone; to her, they no longer existed.

It's curious that Frank Lloyd Wright was nothing like his mother's family. The Lloyd Jones brothers were big and brawny but he was small and light, so much like his father. Like William he was handsome, intelligent, witty, a natural orator and a great musician. But Frank never acknowledged his father's heritage, not even the plain fact that William's gifts had encouraged him to be a remarkable pianist. He never learned to read music but he had an extraordinary ear, and for the rest of his life music was an integral art of Frank's life. But never a word about his father.

Most lives have patterns that turn up many times. Denying anyone's influence is a pattern you can see throughout Wright's life. Over and over he denied getting any idea, style, shape, or method from any other person. Everything came from the miraculous mind of Frank Lloyd Wright. Other architects were influenced by him, he proclaimed, but he was never influenced by them. He denied being influenced by world events or discoveries. Wright believed that he was a pure spring of original thoughts.

It's impossible not to admire his brass certainty and loud praise of himself. No one is immune from influences, good and bad. Other artists acknowledge the influence of teachers and examples—not Frank! Consistently he claimed total originality with his rogue's grin.

In contrast to the dark anxiety of his family home, there was the soft light of the Lloyd Jones valley. The gentle hills of Wisconsin, the growing seasons, and the clean, crisp winters delighted Wright. He fell in love with land and weather. The country rhythms of plowing, planting, tending, and harvesting became part of his philosophy.

Growing up in the Lloyd Jones valley made being close to farmland essential to Wright. All his life he was a country architect, even when he built in cities. He wanted all of us to return to our roots in the fields by making our houses and even our cities part of the forests and farms.

But he was not a happy farmer.

Frank was enchanted by the abstract beauty of nature—blossoms and sunsets—but repelled by cow dung and dirty work.

Anna, a seasoned farm girl, almost worshipped her handsome son, but feared that he was becoming too soft. In the summers she sent Frank to Brother James. (All the Lloyd Joneses were called "brother" or "sister," and Frank continued addressing friends in this way through his life.) At Brother James's farm, Frank's blond curls were cut short, overalls replaced his dapper clothes. He rose at four in the summer dark to help milk the cows. He described farm work as "adding tired to tired and adding it again."

The beauties of nature described in poetry sounded fine, but grunting hogs and clucking chickens didn't sound as good or smell as sweet. Real life on a farm had too much sweat, blood, and dirt.

Frank tried to run away many times. The Lloyd Jones clan was sensible, tough, and content with the gritty needs of farm life. They brought him back and set him to work again.

Dark and light. Adoration from his mother, friction between Frank and his father. The tense house in the city of Madison for the winter, the beautiful valley in the summer. But this wasn't a simple good/bad situation: the anxious winter house was a place of rest, books, and music, while the beautiful summer farm was a place of labor and long hours.

Music was a light in his boyhood and through his life. At seven he pumped the organ while his father practiced. In his autobiography Wright expands this simple chore to a cruel punishment, something like being a galley slave. But the music must have seeped into him through the organ pump handle. Wright became a gifted pianist who always had expensive (usually unpaid-for) grand pianos wherever he lived. In the narrow periods between Anna Wright's tantrums the family would sing around the piano.

Anna was larger than her husband by several inches. There were periods of deep depression when she locked herself in her room for days. Then she flew into violent rages. She shouted at William, threw things, called him names, beat him, and eventually refused to be near him.

The Lloyd Jones clan understood that she was not a mentally healthy woman and decided on a practical, though stern, family solution: they asked William to move away. The gentle man understood that it was the best he could do for his younger children. He packed a few books and instruments and left. He did not abandon his wife and children but was sent away in deep sadness. Frank was about sixteen. A few years later William heard that Anna was accusing him of desertion. To set the record straight and protect his reputation, William asked for a legal divorce. The court agreed that Anna had abused him, and the marriage was ended in 1885.

Frank never saw his father again. Though William had been loving and kind, Frank refused any connection with him for nineteen years. William Wright died in 1904, when Frank—still stubbornly blaming his father for the family's troubles—was thirty-seven years old. His half brothers and sister tried to contact him several times, but he saw them only once, many years later. Like Anna, Frank could erase people from his thoughts without difficulty.

In his autobiography—perhaps even in his mind—it was his father, not his mother, who had become stern and angry. No one else—not William's friends, his other children, nor even the Lloyd-Joneses—saw him this way, yet Anna's violent behavior was obvious to everyone. Still, the autobiography retells Anna's tale of William deserting his family and concocts a fairy-tale reason for William's desertion: because Anna concentrated all her attention and affection on Frank.

It's true that Anna was obsessed by her beautiful son. She spoiled him, gave him special treats, dressed him like a young lord, and praised him constantly. *An Autobiography* tells us that his mother hung framed pictures of great cathedrals on the walls of his nursery so her infant son could absorb their beauty. She was determined that he would become a great architect!

The truth, once again, is less romantic. In their tiny house Frank didn't have a nursery, and it's doubtful if Anna hung the prints of cathedrals on any wall.

Frank's belief in the prints are probably a storyteller's way of emphasizing his mother's devoted attention, which was real enough.

One concrete thing Anna did for her son was encourage his interest in art. As a teacher, she had discovered the German educator Friedrich Froebel. He had devised a fine way of interesting children in graphic patterns and geometry: a system of shapes in fascinating wooden tiles—squares, triangles, circles, bars, arcs. He called them the Froebel Gifts. Anna found a set of the Gifts for Frank and also stocked his playroom with colored paper, paste, pencils, and cardboard. The shapes of those Gifts stayed with him. The pleasure of drawing seeped into his fingers. The stark beauty of geometry lodged in his eyes.

Anna stayed with Frank constantly all her life, wherever he went, seldom living more than a few hundred yards away. Her clinging, day-by-day attention never faltered. Neither did her arguments and interference. He praised his mother publicly, but she irritated and exasperated him. He let his sister Jane care for her when she was old. When she died he didn't bother to attend the funeral.

• 2 •

FOUNDATIONS

EVERY ARCHITECT LEARNS that the first and most important part of a building's structure is its foundation, its level and secure connection to the earth. The rest of the structure is connected to this strong base. The strength of a building depends on it.

To the Lloyd Jones clan, learning was a foundation for the future. In this, Frank was a disappointment.

Anyone could see that he was smart, and he read every book he could find. But he was a hopeless student. His grades were awful. In high school he dropped out of school repeatedly. His mother and aunts—all teachers—encouraged him to work harder. Without a good record, how could he enter a good university?

This practical logic didn't persuade him. Most of

all, following someone else's path didn't appeal. He was offended that teachers would tell him what and how to learn.

At eighteen Frank Lloyd Wright (he had changed his middle name to reflect his part in the Welsh clan) dropped out of high school for the last time, without graduating. His record of grades and attendance was a ruin. He had decided, however, that he was going to become an architect. Ignoring the guidelines and requirements for students at the University of Wisconsin at Madison, he entered as a "special student." Without discipline or study skills, it was predictable that he would bomb.

In his autobiography, Wright suggests that he attended the University of Wisconsin in engineering studies for over three years, dropping out just before graduation because the degree simply wasn't important to him.

What wasn't important to him was the education itself. He dropped out after three *semesters*, little more than a year, failing in most of his classes. The only degrees Frank Lloyd Wright ever received were honorary doctorates, many years later. He entered the profession of architecture without a thimbleful of architectural education. As strange as it seems to us, his ignorance may have been a lucky break.

To understand Frank Lloyd Wright and how much he accomplished, we need to understand how architecture stood just before 1900.

Mark Twain and Dudley Warner called this period the Gilded Age. They probably meant that we were showing off to Europe that America was no longer a crude backwoods culture; however, our attempts at elegance achieved merely fake, shallow opulence. Our culture was gilded, not gold. The dress and design of the time were heavy with decoration, ruffles, details. Nothing escaped decoration—silverware, stoves, clocks, toilets. Most decoration was in the "classic" style, using symbols and themes from Rome, Greece and Egypt.

At that time architecture was also "classic." Its forms came from antiquity. Great blocky buildings rose on American streets, unlike anything in Rome, but their surfaces were crowded with Roman columns, arches, details, and vases copied from ancient ruins.

The architecture of the late nineteenth century had rules of style, and the authority was a school in Paris, the École des Beaux-Arts. The "best" architects of Europe, Britain, and America were educated there. Their work was similar and shared a basic approach.

Most public buildings were built up in layers that represented the march of architectural fashion from Greece to Rome. The layers expressed "orders" of style. The Doric order on the bottom was the oldest and had least decoration. The Ionic order was next. It carried more decoration and its columns had *capitals*—sculptured forms at their tops. Above Ionic and Doric, the Corinthian order was the fanciest, its columns capped with complex sculptures of stone leaves. Designing a building like this was a problem in fitting the orders and their parts to the size and function of the structure, inside and out. A nineteenth-century architect might take great pride in adapting the style and details of ancient Roman baths in Taranto to a courthouse in Zanesville, Ohio.

For residential architecture—homes—the style book had a few more pages. In the United States some native styles had developed—the New England saltbox and Cape Cod cottage, the southwestern adobe, the sod house of the Great Plains, the "shotgun" house in the South. But these common homes were beneath the concern of society architects. They had their own list of classic styles: Greek Revival, Romanesque, Tudor, Queen Anne. Prospective homeowners chose a style that reflected their tastes or their position in society and hired architects who specialized in that style.

Most of the "great homes" in the United States were based on ancient designs. George Washington's beautiful home, Mount Vernon, was a wooden structure designed to look like a Greek stone structure. Monticello, Jefferson's delightful home, was designed in brick and wood using Greek and Roman features.

The theory was that architecture had reached its perfection in Greece and Rome. The best that could be hoped was that a new building would share some of the old classic grace. Architectural historians wrote about the divine harmony in classic architecture, the balance between simple forms and complex repetition of patterns.

In some ways they were right. There *was* harmony and balance, because the Romans and Greeks built sensibly with the materials they had—stone, brick, wood, iron, bronze, lead, and *pozzolana*, a natural concrete found around volcanoes. There were simple limits to what these materials could do. The limits dictated the proportions and the structure of the buildings. Roman architecture and materials couldn't produce an unbroken wall of windows; if many windows were needed, however, the Romans could build a charming series of arches.

There was a deep beauty to these old structures because logic—which was really the limitations of structure and materials—drove the design. Anyone could see the beauty as a feeling of intuitive order.

Earlier in the century, the historian Friedrich von Schelling in his *Philosophie der Kunst* had described architecture as "frozen music." The old builders created a rhythm using the "beat" of simple materials. That rhythm in ancient buildings still appeals to us today.

What late-nineteenth-century architects missed is that materials were changing.

New, booming factories were producing miles of steel beams. Glass was being made in bigger, stronger sheets. Pozzolana wasn't being dug out of volcanic mountainsides, now; better, cheaper cement was being made by the ton in factories. The old limits and the old logic had changed. Architecture hadn't.

A new century was coming. The United States, no matter how much it wanted to be like Europe, was a new society with new ideas. Just how different and how much alike it was would become apparent in 1897, when a miraculous white city was built in Chicago.

Eleven years before that, in 1886, Frank Lloyd Wright was failing to acquire a college education, but he had three razor-sharp tools.

He had an intuitive feel for geometry. Perhaps all the years with the Froebel Gifts had built a marvelous geometric computer in his mind.

He had a wonderful ability to draw and a fascination with color. As a solitary boy he had spent hour upon hour drawing, mostly with colored pencils. For the rest of his life, his best hours were spent with a pencil in his hand.

He had the gift of gab. Words delighted him. He was an avid reader and he was a keen listener when his uncle Jenkin Lloyd Jones preached to his Unitarian congregation. He perceived that words could influence people. He played with words and their rhythm.

He talked and drew so well that while he was flunking out of the University of Wisconsin, he was working for the dean of engineering, Allan Conover. Later that year, just before he abandoned his formal education completely, he talked himself into a job with the architectural firm of Joseph Lyman Silsbee. Silsbee was a Lloyd Jones family friend and was designing the Unity Chapel for Uncle Jenkin. Frank was allowed to make the working drawings for the chapel.

Architectural working drawings are not pretty pictures. They are geometry at work. These drawings make legal statements: they decree exactly the size, shape, and placement of every stick of wood and brick in a building. They are the unforgiving directions for constructing a building in precise, measured, unmistakably clear lines.

One drawing can't describe a building. Hundreds of individual drawings specify the width and depth and height of rooms, the placement of structural beams, the pattern of wooden floors, the plumbing inside walls, the number of shingles for every foot of roof surface.

Architectural drawings look at a building and its parts from many directions—from above, in *plan* view, and from the sides, in architectural views called *elevations*.

These drawings even look in ways your eye can't: a *section* is an imaginary way of seeing, a drawing of how a building or room or piece of wooden window trim *would* look if you cut it, opened it, and looked inside. In a horizontal section view through an orange, you would see a circle for the outside of the peel, another circle inside it, where the orange peel stops, and the triangular sections of fruit inside. Section views make their imaginary cuts vertically, horizontally, or at an angle. If you cut through an ice-cream cone vertically, it would look like a triangle; if you cut it horizontally, it would look like a circle. All these ways of looking and drawing are necessary to describe exactly the way a building should be built.

The elevations show the walls outside and inside the building. Sections through the walls show what's behind the surface—pipes and wires and posts. Plans show how the rooms relate to one another, where doors and steps are. The drawings are numbered and lettered. An elevation of a wall may show a line labeled with the note "sec 10-F," meaning that there is a

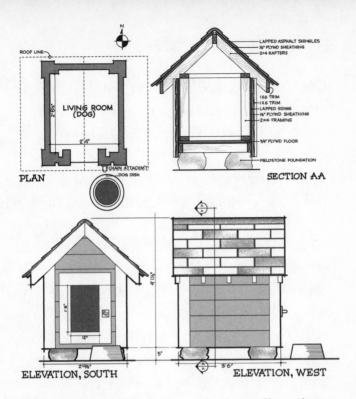

PLAN

LIVING ROOM
(DOG)

ROOF LINE

2'4"

2'5¼"

CHAIN ATTACHM'T
DOG DISH

N

SECTION AA

LAPPED ASPHALT SHINGLES
½" PLYWD SHEATHING
2×4 RAFTERS

1X6 TRIM
1X6 TRIM
LAPPED SIDING
½" PLYWD SHEATHING
2×4 FRAMING

¾" PLYWD FLOOR

FIELDSTONE FOUNDATION

ELEVATION, SOUTH

2'9½"

12"

1'6"

4'1½"

5'

ELEVATION, WEST

3'6"

section view showing what's inside this wall on sheet 10, drawing F.

To some people this jungle of lines and numbers, notes and measurements, is wildly confusing. To Frank it was as simple as eating pie. He had a genius for seeing geometry. The geometry showed him the space as clearly as you see the words on this page. Drawings spoke to him plainly, calmly, and he was never confused. He looked at drawings and understood how things went together. The Unity Temple drawings he made for Joseph Silsbee were complete and logical, drawn with a crisp confidence. Silsbee hired him.

Wright's giant ego was scornful of many polite notions. Loyalty was one of them. In his single-minded world there were only people who could help him and people who stood in his way. He felt that he'd learned all he could from Silsbee. In 1888, after less than a year, he used examples of the work he'd done in the Silsbee office to wangle his way into a position at one of Chicago's cutting-edge architectural offices: Adler and Sullivan. Wright wanted a showcase for his genius. He found something better: a teacher.

Dankmar Adler offered little that Wright desired. He was a fine engineer, quiet and intelligent, who created imaginative structural solutions—clever ways to make buildings strong and stable. He had a special gift for acoustical engineering—managing the sound within an auditorium or concert hall so that the piccolo and the kettle drum could be heard with equal ease from every seat in the house. He was also the "social" partner at Adler and Sullivan, with contacts at the moneyed levels of Chicago society, the best list of potential clients. These practical qualities didn't speak to Wright.

The partner who fascinated him was Louis Henry Sullivan. This was the first person Wright had met whose brilliance, will, and creative fire blazed brighter than his own. Only twenty-eight, Sullivan was already a force in Chicago's renaissance.

A disastrous fire had nearly wiped out the city in 1871. A building boom followed to replace what had been lost. Chicago was a new kind of American city, far from the European connections and stylists of New York and Boston. It was a Midwestern city on a windy plain beside an interior sea. Chicago seemed to demand its own style. Sullivan was eager to provide it.

Boston-born, he was raised by parents who taught dance and followed the arts. He left school at sixteen and passed a rigorous test to enter the first architectural school in the United States at Boston's famous Massachusetts Institute of Technology.

MIT disappointed Sullivan. He was looking for something more than tastefully decorated copies of old buildings. Frustrated, he left school after a year. He worked as a *draftsman* (someone who produces measured, careful architectural drawings) for a time, then set out for Paris to study at the source of architectural "wisdom," the École des Beaux-Arts. He left after a single project, disgusted. Sullivan traveled in Europe, trying to understand the shapes and sense beneath the decorations of ancient buildings. When he returned, he was hired by the colorful Philadelphia architect Frank Furness.

Follow the life of any artist and you will see the early influences that shape later work. Furness was a traditional architect, following the classic styles that Sullivan rejected, but his interest in a British movement called Arts and Crafts that stressed "naturalism" and the harmony in repetitive decoration became part of Louis Sullivan.

Sullivan left Philadelphia for Chicago and a job with William Le Baron Jenney, another factor in Sullivan's style. Jenney recognized that a city was a kind of fireplace. One log doesn't burn well by itself, but many logs together make a hot, blazing fire. Cities brought thousands of businesspeople together. They shared the fire of ambition and profit. Jenney realized that a hotter, more productive city shouldn't spread *out* but *up*. A tall building was meant for business. Its stacks of offices and services could make a city compact and dense. More people at the center of the city shared more creative heat.

Because new buildings no longer depended on thick masonry walls for their strength but on steel structural beams, the city architect could build up. And up. Jenney had invented the skyscraper.

Louis Sullivan studied the skyscraper with his sharp, analytic mind. He saw it as a building with three parts: a base, with public spaces, meeting places and shops; a tall shaft, with stacks of offices sharing the building's services—heat, electricity, telephone and telegraph lines; and a cap, where the building's mechanical services were housed—motors and winches that ran the elevators, big fans that circulated air, main electric switches, and major plumbing valves.

The importance of Sullivan's analysis of the skyscraper is that he didn't cover its three parts over with a blanket of classic columns, arches, and vases. He had a vision: new needs should shape new buildings. Architecture should express what a building did and how it worked. He used a famous phrase to express this shaping process: "Form ever follows function." The form of a good building should show what the building does, what it's about. He insisted that an architect should understand what a building *wanted to be*.

Sullivan's skyscrapers—with structural strength insured by Adler's engineering—expressed all three parts. The base was massive, with strong shapes, often arched. Its shop windows and entrances said, "Look through here!" and "Enter here!" Above his heavy earth-bound base rose the shaft. Sullivan pulled back the usual decorative ledges between floors and emphasized the vertical structure and the building's impressive height. Far up at the top, a cap spread out like the serif at the top of a capital I: a graceful visual end to the shaft, expressing the separate functions of the mechanical services at the top.

A kind of magic bound the strong shapes and distinct parts together: Sullivan's breathtaking artistry with intricate, flowing, naturalistic decoration. He was a master at twining floral and leaf patterns, lifting them up off the surface of the material in three dimensions, and creating rhythmic patterns using repeated blocks of material: cast iron, cast structural pottery called *terra cotta*, and carved stone.

In Sullivan, Frank Lloyd Wright found a teacher

who could train his mind. Sullivan's diagnostic thinking became Wright's design school. How do spaces and shapes relate to one another? How do people move through architecture? What makes harmony between a building and the people who live in it? How can a building's *program*—the purposes, site, restrictions, and budget—shape its form?

In Sullivan, Wright also found his match in ego. Sullivan was famously hot-tempered. Dankmar Adler spent a lot of time soothing rich clients' feelings. Sullivan was brilliant, impatient, arrogant, charming, outspoken, easily insulted, and completely submerged in his work. Architecture consumed his life.

In Wright, Sullivan found a disciple apparently willing to soak up Sullivan's wisdom and take his orders. Wright was clever, quick to understand Sullivan's directions. He lacked architectural experience but had that uncanny ability to understand spaces and geometry. When he was hired, the firm was working hard on the most important structure it had designed, the Auditorium Building. It was filled with thousands of Sullivan's ornamental details, and Wright immediately grasped his style and made the working drawings that guided artisans who would create them.

Architects make a distinction between a picture of a building, called a *rendering*, and measured drawings to guide a building's construction, called *working drawings*. Wright had extraordinary drawing skills to render ornaments, details, rooms . . . anything. And the way he arranged and produced working drawings was logical and crisp. Soon, he was directing other draftsmen working on the same building. In a few years, he became the chief draftsman at Adler and Sullivan, supervising thirty others. Many draftsmen who were more experienced and better educated objected. Wright was younger, cocky, dressed like a dandy, and he was treated like a teacher's pet by Sullivan. They probably groaned when Wright began to address Sullivan as *lieber Meister* ("dear master" in German).

Perhaps Wright was sincere. He certainly learned a major part of his art from Louis Sullivan. Wright and Sullivan were alike in many ways. Both burned a little too brightly for most people. Both thought of themselves as a cut above the rest. Both were intellectual snobs. In his time at Adler and Sullivan, Wright committed himself to the same obsession that drove his *lieber Meister*: architecture became his life.

Suddenly, Frank Lloyd Wright was a fashionable young man with good prospects in a growing city. He had an excellent job, and he meant to enter Chicago society. He courted Catherine Tobin. He was twenty-two; she was eighteen. Her father, a wealthy businessman, thought his daughter was too young to wed and Wright was too flighty to make a good husband, but they were married in 1889. Wright borrowed $5,000 from Sullivan (a vast sum in 1889) and bought property in an almost-rural suburb of Chicago, Oak Park.

The next day, Hannah Wright bought the property next door.

Wright designed a home for himself, based on houses designed by the great Boston architect H. H. Richardson. He had not yet developed his own style.

Frank and Catherine—called Kitty—became the beautiful young couple of Oak Park, hosting dinners, parties, musical evenings, discussions. They threw themselves into the social current and into family. Soon Catherine was pregnant with the first of their six children. Hannah lived next door, never far away, always a part of Frank's life and always ready to criticize his young bride. But they lived with great style, well beyond their finances.

Wright had become indispensable to Sullivan. Friends said he had become "Sullivan's pencil," the tool with which he made his thoughts into designs. Together, they were doing great work. Unfortunately, their relationship probably harmed Sullivan's bond with Adler, since both Wright and Sullivan regarded engineers (like Adler) as old-fashioned fussbudgets.

Residences were never of great interest to Sullivan. He could express the nature of a bank or an auditorium, but he was never able to design an architectural "machine" to express togetherness and warmth. He left residence design—including his own home and his vacation home on the coast of Mississippi—to Wright.

Wright began to use his *lieber Meister's* analysis of what a building *wanted* to be. What did a house do? What were its parts? How did its structure relate to the people inside? What feelings inside the house wanted to be seen in the house's outer form? Wright was beginning to receive credit for his designs: Sullivan named him the co-designer of a prominent Chicago home for industrialist James Charnley.

In 1890, after three years in construction, Adler and Sullivan's Auditorium Building opened. It was immediately celebrated as a victory for a new, truly American architecture. It wasn't a copy of any European model, and its sheer size made European buildings seem small. One of the largest structures in the world at the time, it enclosed eight million cubic feet, a complete hotel of four hundred rooms, over a hundred offices, and a huge concert theater for an audience of 4,200. Sullivan's genius was in every detail. He was especially praised for his understanding of an infant medium: incandescent light. In an age accustomed to gas lights, he designed beautiful fixtures for Edison's fairly new electric lightbulbs and placed them in hidden baffles to bring out the best in his wonderful decoration. The Auditorium established Adler and Sullivan as the leading firm in Chicago at a time when the city was about to astonish the world.

• 3 •

THE WHITE CITY

AN ENORMOUS ARCHITECTURAL event was coming together in Chicago. It would be for American architecture what the Norman invasion or the discovery of the New World was for history: a point of reference in time. It would be a kind of showdown, too, between the old architecture and the new.

The World's Fair of Paris in 1889 had been a great cultural event meant to impress the world with France's power and wealth. A fantastic structure designed by a young French engineer as the enormous symbol of that fair still stands: the Eiffel Tower.

The relatively young United States was impatient to announce itself as a world power. Thirty years after

A view down the waterslide in the White City, the Chicago World's Fair of 1893.

the Civil War, it had bound up its wounds, and linked the width of its continent with rails and telegraph lines. It was a two-ocean nation with immense room for expansion, incalculable mineral resources, and a growing reputation for innovation. Its navy was formidable; its wealth was vast. It was time to insist that this nation was the cultural, intellectual, and industrial peer of any European nation. Many American cities bid for the right to host the 1893 World's Fair, but a syndicate of Midwestern businessmen brought the fair to Chicago with a promise of $8,000,000 in finances.

If Chicago was to present the country in its best light and astonish all of Europe (as well as millions of American visitors), the fair had to be more than a hodgepodge of unrelated exhibits and buildings. One man's vision was the heart of the fair: architect Daniel Burnham was the reassuring pivot around which dozens of distinguished American architects and artists—including Louis Sullivan and Frank Lloyd Wright—would swing. "Uncle Dan" saw the possibility of a holy city: a place of light, harmony, and order, of style and sense. Only a man with a deep philosophical belief in the power of mathematical organization could look at a muddy stretch of Lake Michigan shoreline and see the possibilities of a true (if temporary) utopia.

Burnham gathered his creators—architectural firms like McKim, Mead and White, W.L.B. Jenney, George B. Post, Peabody and Sterns, Henry Ives Cobb, Adler and Sullivan. They began the designs for the separate theme buildings—Transportation, Agriculture, Arts, and others. The landscape planner was Frederick Law Olmstead, who had designed New York's Central Park. The sculptural consultant was Augustus Saint-Gaudens.

The style was to be Beaux Arts Greek and Roman. As a unifying element, the main building blocks for each structure were to have a height of sixty feet. The color was to be white. Burnham planned a gleaming city of white walls and columns, sculptures and arches, like the white marble of ancient Rome, like a dream of heaven.

Burnham also decided the building material: *staff*. This was a cheap and rapid way to create temporary structures. Light wood timbers and wood strips made up the shapes of buildings; then they were covered with rough jute fabric soaked in plaster of Paris. The fabric could be stretched as a surface or pushed wet into molds to make fanciful decorations, sculptures, even monumental vases. Staff was waterproof and versatile, an appropriate material for buildings intended to have a useful life of only a few years. The entire White City was built in twenty-four months.

It was a wonder, laid out in the grand scale of imperial Rome, gleaming in the sunlight. At night, it was even more impressive. It was a showcase for an alternating-current system established by Nikola Tesla, the first all-electric city, blazing with hundreds of thousands of lightbulbs, wired to its own steam power plant. A lagoon reached in from Lake Michigan past Augustus Saint-Gauden's giant gilded statue *Republic*, a Chicago version of the Statue of Liberty. The lagoon created an orderly waterfront for the central buildings. Charming bridges crossed the lagoon and made its little island accessible. Venetian gondolas, electric launches, and steam ferries navigated it. The exquisite landscaping was kept in trim by a legion of caretakers. Crime was suppressed by an on-site police force. Looming above the grand buildings was the engineering marvel of its day and one of the fair's symbols: an immense wheel-like structure reinforced with steel cables pivoting on an enormous axle, lifting room-sized viewing gondolas two hundred and fifty feet into the sky above the White City, designed by and named for its young American engineer—the Ferris wheel.

The White City offered visitors exhibits, education, entertainment, ballyhoo, and glimpses of distant cultures. There were transplanted villages from Africa, Austria, Germany, Ireland, Egypt, Turkey, Lapland, and Java. Visitors could see Hungarian, Algerian, and Chinese theater, ascend in a balloon, ride an ice railway, or watch Little Egypt dance the infamous Hootchy-Kootchy. Beside the sober national exhibits, the visitor could feast on noise and fast food along the Midway, the fair's entertainment sector. It was the first time Americans sampled Aunt Jemima Syrup, Cracker Jacks, Cream of Wheat, Shredded Wheat, and Juicy Fruit gum. At the Chicago World's Fair, America was introduced to the hamburger. More than twenty-seven million visitors came to the fair and went away enthused about a new technological and scientific future.

In ways that can't be calculated, the Chicago World's Fair established the United States as one of the great modern nations. In a similarly powerful way, the style Uncle Dan Burnham had established as its basis, the Beaux-Arts Style, was confirmed as the standard of public buildings for half a century.

One building in the White City wasn't white: Louis Sullivan's Transportation Building. The massive structure was plainer, and expressed in bolder shapes than its Beaux-Arts neighbors. The dominant entrance was a set of telescoping arches covered in gold leaf. The arches' curves radiated as bands of Sullivan's naturalistic decoration. The predominant colors beside the gold of the entrance were earthy reds, oranges, and yellows.

To Sullivan, the White City was a sham. The wood-and-plaster copies of Greek and Roman stone architecture were admissions that America had failed to find its own style. The popular success of the fair was an artistic tragedy to Wright's *lieber Meister*, who said, "This will set American architecture back fifty years."

The bulk of the fair's physical architecture was gone five years later. The buildings had been scheduled for demolition but most of them burned. The hollow wood structure of staff acted like a self-destructive chimney. Only two buildings survive. You may see them today on the site of the White City. The Columbian Museum, originally built of staff, rebuilt in stone, is now the Museum of Science and Industry. The World's Congress Auxiliary Building is now the Art Institute of Chicago.

But you may see the effects of the White City in a larger and more monumental setting. Burnham recruited many of the White City's architects to recreate the nation's capitol in the following years. Burnham designed Union Station, Washington's train depot. Charles McKim completely renovated the White House. Olmstead conceived the settings for the Lincoln Memorial, the Tidal Basin, and the Jefferson Memorial, as well as Rock Creek Park. The commission dominated by the White City Beaux-Arts architects dictated the look of the National Archives Building, the Supreme Court, and the Memorial Bridge. The formal center of Washington, D.C., is built in the image of Chicago's White City, in a permanent but equally counterfeit form. The capitol's major buildings are all transplanted copies from long dead cultures. They assume a borrowed respectability as "official" and "proper" architecture.

Sullivan was right.

How did the White City affect Frank Lloyd Wright? It changed his perceptions as an artist and an architect.

The fair was a watershed in the life of the United States, a point where directions change. And it was a watershed for Wright's work. His aesthetic changes were intense.

Though Wright despised the Classical style of the fair, he was deeply impressed with the power of Olmstead's site-planning, the way the buildings were arranged to create public spaces between them and the way he used water as an element. Olmstead created the lagoon as both a barrier and a highway. It conjured the illusion of great distances within the site. Its movement and reflecting properties became part of the architecture. Wright would always be intensely aware of the possibilities of a site. He would wring every advantage from the landscape's rise and fall, its foliage and open places. Whenever possible, he would use water as a primary element in his site-planning.

Seeing the White City buildings made of staff rise so swiftly made the young man wary of traditional building methods. If large and sturdy structures could be made with sticks, fabric, and plaster, cheaply and swiftly, why weren't architects taking advantage of the possibilities? For the rest of his life, Wright would search for inexpensive, quick, unusual building solutions. He rummaged through hundreds of new building materials as they became available, often using them in ways they were never meant to be applied. Some of his inventions and innovations were surprising, like walls made of skim plaster over thin boards sandwiched around roofing tar paper, half as thick as conventional walls and much less than half as expensive. Some of his material innovations failed or leaked, needing replacement with more common stuff. But he was always suspicious that standard building methods were substitutes for plain thinking and creative solutions.

In the Fine Arts Buildings at the White City, Wright was introduced to a lifelong passion: Japanese woodblock prints. The old images of Hiroshige and Hokusai were a revelation to him. Their serene compositions, strong light and dark contrasts, and vivid colors had been made a century before, but they seemed so fresh and contemporary! Japanese art became an obsession with Wright, almost a second career. Few were aware that he was a respected collector of and authority on Japanese art. In lean times, he frequently eked out a living by trading in Japanese prints.

One of the most important effects of the White City on Frank Lloyd Wright came from the short trip across an Olmstead bridge to the little island in the lagoon. There he found a half-scale version of a thirteenth-century Japanese temple, Ho-o-den, built as part of the Japanese exhibit. In contrast to the plaster Roman counterfeits and the hurly-burly of the Midway, this temple in a glade seemed entirely natural, a world apart. It was constructed simply but with exquisite craftsmanship of unpainted wood. Its floors were woven-grass tatami mats. Its walls were rice-paper screens or rectangles of plain white plaster. Its roof of shallow angles was modest but firm, echoing the gentle topography of the earth beneath it, embracing and protecting the visitor with broad overhangs.

In later years, Wright would deny the influence of Japanese architecture as a seed of his Prairie Style, in windows, walls, screens, and many other distinctly Wright features. But this is a comfortable thing about a rogue and grand old faker like Wright: he almost invites us to make our own conclusions, since we know his are so seldom honest.

Around this time, Uncle Dan Burnham saw Wright's immense talent and intelligence. One of Burnham's gifts was an ability to judge character. He saw, correctly, that Wright needed discipline and education. To Burnham there was an obvious solution, and he made the young man a spectacularly generous offer: he would pay for a complete education including expenses at the École des Beaux-Arts in France for four years, support Wright's growing family while he was away, and guarantee him a job in what was now the premier architectural firm in the United States on his graduation.

With equally spectacular arrogance, Wright refused.

Uncle Dan was right and he was wrong: Frank needed discipline—perhaps he never really acquired it. But he didn't need the École des Beaux-Arts. He had learned enough about Beaux Arts style from the White City, and he was already on the far side of his most important watershed.

• 4 •

BOOTLEGGING

FRANK LLOYD WRIGHT had become an important part of the work done by Adler and Sullivan. He directed the flow of working drawings from the firm's draftsmen and was beginning to add his design style to their work.

His new home in Oak Park was a social tool with which he cultivated Chicago society. He and Kitty entertained often and in high style—food, music, art, conversation, and a dazzling mix of guests. It wasn't a home as much as a theater with Frank as the star player and producer, showcasing his brilliance. He even designed Kitty's clothes.

Photos from this time show a dapper young man in his mid-twenties with the raised eyebrows of devilish

Wright, circa 1890–1895.

confidence, dressed in tweeds and high collars. Frank was a clotheshorse. As a boy his mother had dressed him like a fashion illustration. As a young man, he saw no reason to lower his standards. Throughout his life he wore suits and shirts custom made by skillfully flattering tailors. His custom shoes had raised heels to enhance his 5'-8½" height. He dressed carefully in unique style. When Frank Lloyd Wright arrived, everyone knew it.

Rushing headlong and without a second thought into debt, he was undismayed. "Give me the luxuries and let the necessities take care of themselves." He owed tailors, grocers, builders, piano makers, and anyone who would give him credit. Hannah Wright would occasionally try to reform him, and Frank claimed remorse, but true regret just wasn't in him.

Frank Lloyd Wright saw himself as a special category of human being: an artist above common requirements, above the laws and even the morality of normal people.

Ignoring the rules everyone else had to follow ended his time at Adler and Sullivan.

Companies that sell creativity often restrict their

designers' work: all creative output belongs to the company. In architecture, especially, there are usually clauses in a designer's contract that forbid architectural work outside the firm. It's sensible: junior designers shouldn't compete with the office that hired them.

Wright was moonlighting, designing what he called "bootleg" houses outside the Adler and Sullivan office for clients in Oak Park. Why? Later, he claimed that he did it for the money, or to explore residential design. More likely the central reason was Wright's inability to be part of any team. He *was* the team. Breaking with Adler and Sullivan was inevitable. He had learned so much at Sullivan's side and so much from the work of the active architecture office that he had to deny being influenced.

Wright hadn't produced one or two bootleg houses but five, all prominent homes in Oak Park. It was an open challenge to the office's ethical standards and, to Sullivan, an insult. The young man he had hired, trained, given the benefit of his design genius, had betrayed him. Other, less fiery men might have worked out their problems and continued together. Sullivan fired him, furious, shortly after the Chicago World's

Fair opened. Wright and Sullivan didn't speak again for twelve years.

Wright took offices nearby and began his own practice almost immediately, not much affected by being cast out of his *lieber Meister's* studio.

As Sullivan was influenced by Furness and Jenney, Wright was influenced by Sullivan. It's common to note the positive influences on a young artist, but what about the bad influences? Sullivan surely trained Wright's analytic abilities and refined his understanding of how architecture is shaped by function, and Sullivan passed on much of his facility with decoration. But he also set the young man firmly in the role of a prima donna. Sullivan, the poster child for artistic temperament, was a poor example of a patient and workmanlike creator. Wright learned from Sullivan the egotist that "great men" in his profession could act illogically, impolitely, even cruelly, and be excused because of their brilliance. It was an unfortunate lesson he never overcame.

Eighteen ninety-three was a grand year for Chicago's prominence in the world, but it also marked the beginning of a national financial slowdown. Wright took several clients with him from Adler and Sullivan and few new commissions came in.

The slumping economy dissolved the firm of Adler and Sullivan. Louis Henry Sullivan kept the offices in the tower of his great Auditorium Building for as long as he could, then shifted to smaller and smaller spaces in Chicago until he was working out of his own home on small country banks and shops. Dankmar Adler died of a sudden stroke in the spring of 1900. Sullivan never again created grand buildings.

Sullivan's fall had nothing to do with Wright's departure. He destroyed himself with a thorny personality and his refusal to compromise. He began to drink heavily. He was called one of the great figures in American architecture but he had lost everything. He died alone in a Chicago hotel room in 1925. The room had been quietly paid for by more successful architects of the city. They dropped by on the proud man from time to time and secretly left wads of bills in his coat pockets.

Wright was financially down and out many times and went through the country's great and small depressions, but his creative spark never dimmed. He always bounced back because he always expected to. Wright's ego was stronger than Sullivan's. It may be that great artists—even patient, workmanlike artists—need a toughness of mind that is rare.

Wright had something else that Sullivan lacked: he was perennially enthused, delighted at each new day, and unwaveringly charming. Sullivan's ego was a wall; Wright's was a stage.

• 5 •

A PRAIRIE WIND

WRIGHT SOON MOVED his office from downtown Chicago to a newly built space in his Oak Park home. It was now more than a social theater; it was a business address and an architectural laboratory where he experimented with new techniques as he added to the structure.

In his bootleg houses and in his new work there were hints of a style Wright was inventing. He believed, with Sullivan, that a uniquely American architecture should rise out of American influences. But the style came slowly, and he began with homes in fashionable "old school" styles—Queen Anne, Neo-Colonial, Dutch Colonial, Tudor. Even in these early fashion pieces he struggled to simplify organization within the house.

Most conventional homes were designed like a set of blocks—one room, one block. They were boxes connected to one another by doors, jumbled into an overdecorated outside box which announced its exterior style. A "proper" home had dozens of cramped, dim rooms—the vestibule, the foyer, the parlor, the drawing room, the butler's pantry. Shouldn't there be a way to simplify homes?

The Arts and Crafts movement was a strong factor in Wright's emerging style. It was more than a look; it was a philosophy. The kernel of Arts and Crafts theory was the belief that the Industrial Age had taken men from their home jobs and installed them as faceless workers in factories. The sacred family bond had been shattered. Rows of workers' houses were thrown up on virtually identical plans. Machines turned out tons of decorated bric-a-brac. Industrial workers and their families were doomed to sameness. The fresh experience of life had been cheapened or discarded; the center was gone.

The Arts and Crafts answer to this gloomy situation was a return to individual effort, to plain handworked crafts and materials—wood, pottery, fabric, and metal that carried a human warmth in the mark of the maker's hand. Another part of the answer was the reestablishment of the home as a family shrine, centered on the mythic hearth that held a symbolic and actual fire.

Frank Lloyd Wright ate this mystical artistic crusade like catnip. He swallowed it whole and began to lecture on the subject at public forums like Chicago's famous Hull House, founded by the activist urban leader, Jane Addams.

The movement wasn't the same on both sides of the Atlantic. In Britain, Arts and Crafts featured naturalistic wallpaper patterns hand-printed from medieval drawings, plain and sturdy oak furniture made by hand, and iron fixtures cleverly wrought by blacksmiths. Inevitably, these lovely items—custom made by artist-craftsmen—were too expensive for ordinary families. The reality of the Arts and Crafts movement in Britain was beyond the means of the working families it hoped to save. It became a chic look for the fashionably liberal rich.

But American converts to the movement—like Wright, furniture-maker Gustav Stickley, and Uncle

Jenkin Jones, now a nationally prominent preacher—believed that the problems of a modern society could be solved by the technology that created it. To American Arts and Crafts designers the machine itself wasn't evil, only the way it was used. Indeed, the machine could be a gift that allowed a craftsman to amplify his output and place beautiful, practical objects and simple architecture within the grasp of common people.

Several architectural principles of the movement shaped Wright's developing beliefs. Arts and Crafts architects tried to reduce the number of rooms within a house to its functional minimum. These rooms should flow into one another naturally, harmoniously, not as boxes within a box but as interlocking spaces. The building shouldn't dominate its site but grow out of it, expressing an agreement between structure and nature. The materials of the house should be natural and simple, local if possible. Its ornament should be subdued and enhance the natural lines of the structure's form. Most important, every part of the structure—its engineering, materials, decoration, furnishings, fabrics, and colors—should spring from the same artistic idea.

The ideal Arts and Crafts house should make one clear design statement about family, art, and shelter.

These basic American Arts and Crafts principles, renamed "organic architecture," shone brilliantly in Frank Lloyd Wright's architecture for half a century.

But while he was lecturing about Arts and Crafts, the struggle to develop a style of his own created some awkward homes. Yes, the site and the building should be an agreeable partnership, but cramped city lots defied him. Many of his early homes look cranky and completely out of place. Two of his houses from that period, the Blossom and McArthur homes, were designed at the same time in his office. They were built at about the same time on a pleasant suburban street, separated by less than two feet. Yet they shouted in totally different styles that clashed grievously with one another and with everything else on the street. Most of Wright's city-lot homes stood out like greyhounds at a cat show. This caterwauling of styles didn't faze Wright: he was using these ungainly houses as design laboratories, no matter what the consequences were for his clients or their neighborhoods.

This street laboratory worked. Each house was a

step toward a new kind of residential architecture never seen before. Wright was struggling toward the thing that Sullivan missed: a machine for living, an architectural expression of family and warmth and shelter.

There was an irony in his search for the perfect home: Wright was trying to create a family place for a family he never had. Warmth and comfort and harmony were never a part of his boyhood family. With Hannah at its center, the family was out of tune and torn apart by anger and madness. The children of his own growing family, more fixed on Kitty than on their work-obsessed father, never satisfied his need to be the center of that warmth.

Wright was synthesizing: bringing elements from here and there together in a new thought: the White City model of an ancient Japanese temple, the warmth of Arts and Crafts wood, Sullivan's logical forms and graceful decorations—they all came together with his love for the rolling hills of the Lloyd Jones valley.

This style synthesis began to have recognizable parts: low roofs with wide, protective overhangs that suggested shelter; the hearth of a large, central fireplace; natural, local materials with natural colors; spaces that flowed into one another. These new houses

Kitty Wright with Llewellyn, circa 1907.

didn't rise like towers but seemed to flow with the wind off the prairie, blown out parallel to the grassy ground. They were suburban homes; none of them were actually built *on* the broad, lonely prairie. But it's easy to see how they came *from* it. Shallow but substantial masses were laid up in wide, flat brick of a tawny color. Darker horizontal bands of windows paralleled the ground. The flat, sweeping shapes made the trees around them look tall and grand.

The first house that completely developed this new "prairie" style was the Ward Willits home, built in Highland Park around 1901. It was a little like a few earlier Wright homes. The windows were similar to some that Sullivan had designed. The brickwork was familiar, nothing unusual. The roof forms were unremarkable, easy to build. And yet there was no house anywhere that was anything like it. It was arresting in its new kind of beauty.

The inside was even more astonishing. The spaces were open and bright and plain—living room here, dining room there, bedrooms up there—but they were all branch parts of one cozy space. They were set apart not by walls but by clever shifts in the floor and ceiling, by changes of material, by peekaboo screens that invited you to slip behind and beyond them. Any visitor could feel the warmth of wood and delight in the beauty of its grain (always stained, never painted). Plain white or lightly colored plaster wall surfaces were set off by wood strips and bands and by wood *wainscoting* (a band of panels that rise from the floor to mid-wall height). Everything was simple, logical, understandable . . . and delightfully comfortable. You might suspect that the house grew like a tree, all of one piece, from one strong seed.

The Prairie homes, like most later Wright houses, have a special quality. From the outside, they look solid and friendly, but private and a little mysterious, as if they're keeping a secret. And they always have a secret: the clever arrangement of magic spaces inside.

There are many Prairie Style homes, and many early Wright buildings. Between 1894 and 1911, Wright completed 135 commissions. But the benchmark for the Prairie Style may be the Robie House. Some call it one of the turning points in American architecture. Others say it's one of the two most beautiful homes in America. (And, yes, the other is also by Wright.)

Robie was a successful young manufacturer of bicycles who wanted a house without "doodads," simple and straightforward. He wanted privacy and yet wanted to be part of the pleasant suburban site he'd bought. Wright was his man.

It's a big house occupying a long, narrow lot near the University of Chicago. It was completed in 1909, but its design is so pure that it will always seem modern. Wright used one of his favorite tricks for the home's exterior walls: the shallow, reddish brick had

Wright's Robie House, 1909, the benchmark of the Prairie Style.

deeply indented horizontal mortar joints, while the vertical joints were even with the surface; this scored the walls horizontally. The brick walls step back from the street and are capped with grayish-white limestone sills. Dark bands of windows framed by darkly stained wood make a contrast to the brick and limestone. The dark brown roof has a shallow angle and almost unbelievable overhangs. Wright loved to play with the engineering of a *cantilever* (a structure that juts out horizontally from a vertical surface without any other support), and some of his Robie overhang corners are twenty-one feet from the nearest solid wall.

The depth of the overhangs do more than suggest shelter or add to the horizontal feel of the building. It's a mark of Wright's meticulous craftsmanship that he calculated the angles of the sun's summer and winter passage across the Chicago sky. The Robie's overhangs shade the interior from the high, hot summer sun, but welcome what heat the lower-angle winter sun can offer.

Another Wright residential trick is to almost hide the front door. The home doesn't exactly tell strangers to go away, but it does make the entrance confusing enough to insist on privacy.

The Robie interior is typical of the Prairie Style. Wright had a quirky dislike of basements and attics. Most of his homes are built on *slabs*, flat concrete pad foundations. The ground floor is often reserved for play or work rooms. Entering the Robie House, the visitor steps up a formal shallow staircase to the living spaces on the second floor and a higher perspective. On flat ground only a little height will yield a long view, and will also ensure privacy, that sense of safe enclosure. Bedrooms are on the third floor.

The two main spaces, living and dining rooms, are only partly separated by a massive stone fireplace with hearths on both sides. The dining room was one of the Arts and Crafts "holy places," the meeting place of family over meals, the place to welcome guests and share good times. Wright always made his dining rooms happy events.

Soft earth colors, plain *detailing* (the way trim and surfaces are handled), and the natural rhythm of wood grain are everywhere. The stained-glass leaded windows come directly from the Arts and Crafts playbook, but they aren't medieval. Perennially modern, they were designed by Frank Lloyd Wright in his best Froebel Gifts style as repeated geometric compositions abstracted from the shapes and colors of trees. Wright became famous for his thrilling, expressive stained-glass windows. Many of these art-glass windows from demolished buildings now hang in museums. A long bank of these fascinating window units marches along one side of the long living space. Like many of the elements in Wright's architectural world, the windows create both an invitation and a barrier: you look both *through* them and *to* them. Peekaboo was Wright's favorite game.

In the Robie House, Wright was beginning to develop an unmistakable mark of his style: the floors, walls, and ceilings were *modular*—they were measured out in the same shape with the same measurements. The Robie House was built on a grid of exact squares, four feet wide and four feet long. Beams, windows, walls, and doors fit into this grid. These modules are both functional and artistic: standard measurements make the construction easier and quicker; the modules create a visual "beat," a rhythm that gives the inhabitants a sense of order, a reassurance of knowing where things *should* be.

Each Wright house has its own rhythm, based on a module that is a square, rectangle, triangle, or even a hexagon.

Much of the furniture is built in. Larger pieces of movable furniture are designed with the same meticulous decorative artistry Wright gave to the windows, following the Arts and Crafts notion that everything should spring from a common thought. But this is where Wright's genius falters, falls down flat on its face.

Frank Lloyd Wright designed some of the ugliest furniture ever built. Not only was it unattractive, it was dangerous. His chair designs, especially those conceived as planes of laminated wood, had a tendency to suddenly topple over with some minor shift in the sitter's position. Even Wright sometimes fell.

Never one to admit a fault, Wright rationalized that this disastrous instability was good, because it made us aware of our balance.

He also deserves an architectural slap on the hand for his awful kitchens, usually cramped boxes stuffed into a corner outside the traffic pattern of the house. They lack space, ingenuity, attention, and detail. The reason is that Frank Lloyd Wright never cooked a meal in his entire life. He was waited on by his mother and servants all his life. He had no notion of how a kitchen really worked.

Furniture and kitchen aside (the chairs do look fine in photographs), the Robie House is one of America's masterpieces of residential design. Wright was forty-three, and his Oak Park practice was booming. His international reputation was growing. He could afford to design dangerous furniture.

• 6 •

INSTINCT AND WIND

WHILE WRIGHT WAS developing the Prairie Style, an architectural possibility revealed itself at the Lloyd Jones homeplace in Spring Green.

His aunts, Nell and Jane Lloyd Jones, were dedicated teachers. Establishing the Hillside Home School in the Lloyd Jones valley was such an important commitment that they pledged to one another that neither would marry.

They didn't need children of their own: they had Frank. They gave him all their motherly attention, a concerned kindness unlike Hannah Wright's dark lecturing. He was always pleased to help them.

The school needed a reliable year-round water supply, so the Lloyd Jones uncles dug a reservoir into the hill above the school. A windmill and pump were needed to keep it full from their deep prairie well. The obvious solution would have been to erect one of the manufactured windmills sold all over the Midwest, bolted iron contraptions as common as sunflowers. But Nell and Jane were "progressive" educators with a nephew who was becoming famous for his designs. Couldn't he design something prettier than the standard cross-braced derrick for a windmill?

He could and did. Wright invested the same meticulous calculation he used in figuring the sun's winter and summer angles to determine the wind directions and storm patterns that blew down the Lloyd Jones valley. And he exercised what would prove to be, over the next fifty years, an uncanny instinct (without the aid of formal study or higher mathematics) for advanced engineering.

Unconsciously, Wright was following an ancient artistic path. There were no schools of engineering during the Middle Ages and the Renaissance, yet master builders built vast cathedrals that are still standing. Bridges of grace and strength were built and are still standing. Modern engineers are puzzled that any designer could have accomplished such engineering wonders without the aid of computers, steel reinforcement, advanced material physics, calculus, or power equipment.

Successful structure is essentially the balance of forces, and the successful medieval engineers were most often sculptors. The sculptor must have an intuitive understanding of balance and the lines of strain within a form. Engineer-sculptors "saw" the physics of their structures as compositions of mass, tension, and counter-mass.

Modern engineers also pass over the obvious fact that a lot of ancient bridges and churches collapsed, some catastrophically, and many died because of failed engineering. We remember and record only the successes. Frank Lloyd Wright had an admirable number of engineering successes over a very long work life. He is also famous for his failures. But even the pickiest engineers admit that none of his failures were catastrophes: the worst that critics can say about Wright as an engineer is that most of his roofs leaked, or that a few walls needed reinforcing after many years in service.

Wright considered the forces acting on a windmill

and developed a sculptural solution. He took trees as his inspiration: they weren't rigid, so that wind flexed their leaves, twigs, branches, and trunks, distributing the strain throughout the system. They stood so firmly because they had a deep, strong root.

Wright invented a deep foundation to anchor a vertical "trunk" of steel rods, all of them free to bend. Bolted to these rods at regular intervals were horizontal "plates"—we would call them "floors"—each composed of two shapes, a diamond emerging from one face of an octagon. The diamond's point, angled toward the worst storm paths, cut the wind like the prow of a ship. The octagon and the diamond both opposed and supported each other. He covered the tall, slender structure with nothing more substantial than wood and cedar shingles. Light, limber, interactive, it was an elegant solution.

All five Lloyd Jones brothers, practical farmers, were shocked. How could their foolish sisters be gulled by their even more foolish nephew? This gimcrack notion wouldn't stand in a midafternoon summer calm, much less a winter blow straight off of the Great Plains! Their local builder, Cramer, was also shocked. They

want him to build a reed-thin tower sixty feet h
hold up a fourteen-foot whirling propeller!

Wright's aunts sent a telegram to Oak Park: "CRAMER SAYS WINDMILL TOWER SURE TO FALL. ARE YOU SURE IT WILL STAND?"

Wright replied, "BUILD IT."

They built it in 1896. The tower that could not stand has endured winter blasts faithfully for over a hundred years now. In 1938 the shingle cladding was replaced with equally light cedar board-and-batten skin, because it required less care. In 1989 it was disassembled, and some aged parts replaced, and reassembled as designed. It's still standing.

The success of this tiny structure meant a lot to Wright. He had achieved something within his family that won him admiration from his hardheaded Welsh uncles. He'd also proven himself as an innovative engineer who had given himself permission to trust his innate structural instincts. They were strong instincts and seldom failed him.

• 7 •

∫OAP AND GOD

WRIGHT'S REPUTATION WAS growing and his
ego was sprinting out ahead of it. He was eager to
design bigger buildings, businesses, and churches. Part
of his genius was moving in circles where he could
beguile wealthy men and encourage them to commission him.

One of the most colorful figures within the Arts
and Crafts movement was Elbert Hubbard, a businessman, lecturer, and artist. He cut a fine figure in his
oversized soft bow ties, broad black hats, and flowing
capes. Wright, too, began to wear big bow ties, capes,
and his own design for a strange flat hat—something
like a cake on a Frisbee. He took up carrying a cane,
though he never needed its support. It was ceremonial,

a showy tool for pointing grandly and transforming simple walking into a royal progress. He affected these styles from another age for the rest of his life.

Hubbard was more than an "artiste." He was an important figure in the Larkin Company of Buffalo, New York, a mail order manufacturer of soaps and perfumes. He was married to a sister of the company's president, John Larkin. Mail order business accounting and paperwork was complex, but Larkin had a brilliant bookkeeper in Darwin D. Martin. The young man was efficient, intelligent, steady, and enthusiastic about nearly everything.

The company was almost exclusively run by Larkin family members. The accounting department could have been a dead end for Martin. But the flamboyant Hubbard encouraged him to impress John and the other Larkins with innovations and ideas and make himself indispensable. Wright would be Martin's brightest offering to the Larkin Company.

Darwin Martin and his equally enthusiastic brother, W. E. Martin, owned a business in Chicago, the E-Z Polish Company, producing polish for shoes and iron stoves. W. E. wrote to his brother about an exciting young architect he'd met, Frank Lloyd Wright. Wright was building him a house in Oak Park. Darwin should meet him, know him, persuade this genius to build a home for him in Buffalo!

W. E. wrote "[Wright is] about 32 yrs. old. A *splendid* type of manhood. He is not a *freak*—not a 'crank'—highly educated and polished, but no *dude*—a straightforward businesslike man—with high ideals." He went on to describe Wright's experience and education—inflated and fictionalized by Wright. W. E. had been persuaded that Wright was a graduate engineer instead of a three-month dropout and had been far more important at Adler and Sullivan than chief draftsman. W. E. concluded by suggesting, "Can you not manage to have him first *discovered* by Mr. L[arkin]. An office such as Wright can build will be talked about all over the country. It would be an ad that money spent in any other way cannot buy. I am not too enthusiastic in this—he is *pure gold*."

But gold is what Wright had found in W. E. Martin as well, and he worked the friendship like a miner following a vein of ore—from brother to brother, and on through the broad Larkin family. He mined nine large commissions out of this vein, and made a life-long friend and supporter in the steady, loyal person of Darwin D. Martin.

Both Martin brothers looked forward to the houses that Wright would design for them. Both ran smack into the tawny Roman brick wall of Wright's careless attitudes. As the actual building of his house dragged on, the elder and more volatile W. E. complained bitterly and accused Wright of outright fraud, at one point telling his brother, "If he is sane he is *dangerous*." The younger brother, D. D., developed a more workable and affectionate attitude, chiding Wright with cheerfully penned lectures on punctuality, following up on details, meeting his obligations, and so on. He also played the mediator between his infuriated older brother and the proud, easily insulted Wright. In a letter sent to both men he demanded that they recognize both the faults and the virtues in one another and stop quarreling like little boys.

We don't know how D. D. managed to mediate his wife's anger. She saw the prospective home as a dwelling in which she was expected to live, entertain, and raise a family—not as a Frank Lloyd Wright sculpture.

She pleaded for clothes closets, bedrooms of a size that would accept a standard bed, and sensible arrangements for serving dinner. (In Wright's plan, servants bringing food from the kitchen were forced to cross the entry hall to reach the dining room.) Wright simply ignored her requests, as he ignored the requests of most clients' wives.

The simple fact was that he was not interested in his clients' desires. He was providing them an opportunity to live in a work of art created by the great Frank Lloyd Wright; that should be enough. Minor inconveniences were a small price to pay for such glory.

And there were the flowerpots. Wright was obsessed with flowerpots, big ones, five and six feet across, grand enough to be called "urns." He used them to punctuate the long sills of walls and to finish majestic blocks of masonry with a flourish. Lots of flowerpots. Some people didn't understand the need for all those pots, especially clients who hadn't requested the vast, expensive, custom-made concrete cauldrons big enough to sleep in.

W. E. and D. D. moved into Wright houses remarkably unlike one another. W. E.'s house was not the now-recognizable Prairie Style but a tall composition of clean white stucco walls with windows trimmed in dark wood. The roof lines were recognizably Wright, but the massing and the utilitarian planes of the house were more like a style that was intriguing Wright at the time. It began as the Secessionist Style in Vienna, developed by a group of young architects who fascinated Wright with their clean, simple lines. Later this style became known as the International Style. Though Wright filched it originally from the boys in

The D. D. Martin House with two of Wright's decorative urns.

Vienna, he later implied that he started the whole International Style.

D. D.'s house in Buffalo, New York, was a sprawling Prairie Style home, far from the prairie. It was a much-enlarged version of a modest house Wright had designed as a feature for *Ladies' Home Journal*, "A Home in a Prairie Town." Some of Mrs. Martin's objections came from Wright's heavy-handed adjustments in size from the little published bungalow. Many of D. D.'s objections came from Wright's underestimates of cost. Like most Wright homes, the cost of construction had no resemblance to the budget Wright declared at the beginning of the project. For the sprawling house and the little guest house built for Martin's sister and brother-in-law, the final cost was several hundred thousand dollars—millions in present value.

Mrs. Martin was never happy with the house. She thought it was dark and gloomy, poorly laid out for simple living, and much too large. She sold it with some relief soon after D. D. died many years later. Presently being restored to its original (if less-than-logical) splendor, the Martin home is an official National Historic Landmark.

Two larger public buildings were on Wright's drawing boards during this period, both of them startlingly new expressions of architecture. They were remarkably similar in style and look but completely different in purpose.

D. D. had, indeed, introduced Wright to John Larkin. The old man was, of course, mesmerized by Wright's flow of ideas and flattery. At his best, the architect was a kind of oral poet, a Welsh singer of bewitching songs, and one of the most graceful hucksters the United States has ever produced.

The company needed a new headquarters where its large staff would process mail orders. Larkin, a white-bearded, hard-headed businessman, had space on the company's industrial property and stubbornly resisted Wright's persuasions to move the headquarters to the country. Wright was always trying to scare clients out of the wicked city.

Wright was faced with a dismal site, surrounded by factories and railroad switchyards. In the early decades of the twentieth century, this environment was not only dirty but dangerous. Steam was the predominant power. Factories and heavy transportation—railroads—were energized by steam boilers fired by the cheapest available coal. This meant that the air around the company's headquarters would be heavy with soot, sulfur, and the acid products of reactions between sunlight, moisture, and the byproducts of burning coal. If John Larkin stood outside on the future site of his headquarters for an entire day, his white beard would become gray.

The site's challenges led Wright to an entirely new solution, common today but radical for his time. He sealed the building from the noxious environment outside it. He engineered ways to filter incoming air, to cool it using an early form of air-conditioning during the summer, and to provide a healthy, cheerful environment for Larkin employees in the midst of industrial squalor.

A few prime factors guided every part of the design. The interior should create its own "view," using space and—most importantly—light. In the face of factory, street, and railroad grit, the interior should be sparkling clean: washable surfaces, easy to maintain. For health and safety, all building materials should be fireproof. The interior environment should stress Larkin "family" (employee) bonding. The progressive harmony of the Larkin business should be emphasized, along with the efficiency of a crisply run business.

Looking at Wright's solution from our perspective, details of the Larkin building seem unremarkable. This is because his inventions were logical and appropriate. They're used so often today that they're unnoticed parts of our architectural landscape.

One example is his reinvention of toilets. To facilitate frequent, thorough cleaning, Wright designed a new pattern of toilet that bolted to the wall and didn't touch the floor. Toilet stalls were similarly hung from walls and ceiling with open space beneath. We see this pattern everywhere today without recognizing its advantages: mops can swirl under every bowl and cubicle panel freely, without corners to catch dirt and germs.

The Larkin windows were an innovation in themselves: they were *double-glazed* (a sandwich of two panes of glass, like most modern windows). The floors were channeled to carry wires for the recently invented telephone and for relatively new electric lines (standard practice in all offices today). Wall surfaces were light-reflecting glazed tile, easy to wash down. The employees were provided with a cheerful and well-equipped lunchroom so they weren't required to leave the building's protective bubble.

The main workspace was an enormous, uncluttered pattern of built-in steel desks within a sunny atrium. Balconies connecting offices lined the atrium, and the noble space was lit by a grand skylight, providing natural light supplemented by carefully placed stalks bearing the still-new electric bulbs.

The Larkin Building shared something with many of Wright's Prairie Style homes: its interior world was warm and human; its exterior insisted on privacy. In the case of the Larkin Building, the insistence on separation was firm: it looked like a fortress. Its stern, dark brick (dirt-concealing) planes and stark walls rose in a composition of *piers* (tall rectangular blocks), like buttresses for a high bridge that had been stolen away.

Stairs to the balcony offices were moved out into the massive corner piers, and here Wright played his familiar game of peekaboo. At first glance the Larkin Building is a monolithic block, but a closer look reveals that the great corner piers are delicately separated from the central block by a tall slit window of glass. Strong piers that rise from the base terminate in decorative sculptural globes instead of bearing the weight of the roof. What seems, isn't. We're forced to see the Larkin mass differently at second glance, as an intricate arrangement of blocks. Froebel would have been delighted.

The Unitarian Church to which Frank Lloyd Wright belonged had burned down in 1905. The congregation wanted a new church at a good price. They would have been pleased with a white New England chapel capped by a tall steeple rising toward God's heaven. But Wright saw the new church as an opportunity to experiment. He flicked his silver tongue, bewitched the building committee, and set out to design what he chose.

During construction, the congregation of Oak Park Unitarians must have been suspicious. To save money, Wright experimented with a new construction method, concrete successively poured into rising wooden wall molds. When the forms were taken away, each pour left its particular line on the wall planes.

There seemed to be no exterior windows. The outside walls were cold and forbidding, without an obvious entrance.

There were two sections in this urban-lot composition: the chapel and the fellowship hall, which Wright described as a "good-time place" to meet, celebrate, and share joy. The rising chapel began to resemble a prison or an impregnable vault. The space within was almost a perfect cube, and the corners were marked by brooding piers. The Oak Park congregation must have dreaded their daily trips past the building site as the monster grew.

But Wright delighted his fellow Unitarians and Uncle Jenkin with a brilliant interior. It was a new testament in church architecture. Entering through the *pergola* (a covered walkway) between chapel and good-time place, worshippers walked around the core, separated by walls and pierced screens, to one of several entries. There, shallow stairs ushered them up into a magnificently proportioned space that sang with light. It was lit from above by a huge skylight and a band of stained-glass windows at the height of the walls. The cube of space that looked awkward from outside became the logical way to bring the congregation close to the speaker near the center. It was called Unity Temple, and it is one of Wright's most successful early works. It changed sacred architecture, and it stands today as a Chicago landmark.

Against the current of all this success, it's possible to make a few critical observations. The successively poured concrete "bathtub rings" were not well liked. To hide them, ivy was planted quickly and watered often. The corner piers were largely decorative, like the inevitable flower urns. There is a strangely similar form and quality to the Larkin Building and the Unity Temple. They are both arrangements of piers that seem monolithic and then yield to a lighter, slightly more playful interpretation. What a young architecture student might ask is, "Shouldn't the form convey the meaning of the function?" Shouldn't a mail order business look quite unlike a church?

The question is moot. Both buildings were successful expressions of Frank Lloyd Wright, if not soap and God.

Yes, they leaked.

A few years after the turn of a new century, Wright

was charging through a period of almost superhuman creativity, performing miracles of design and fresh sight, perfecting the Prairie Style even as he was leaping to other styles. He was bringing in commissions from the wealthy, living high, evading his creditors, cutting a handsome and rakish figure about Oak Park and Chicago. Neighbors watched him roar past in the "Yellow Devil," his custom-built yellow sports car, wearing aviator's goggles and a leather helmet, sometimes with women other than Catherine Wright. He seemed unbeatable. Nothing could bring him down.

Nothing but the ingenious, intricate, demon-haunted, overburdened, and overworked genius mind of Frank Lloyd Wright.

• 8 •

A FAILURE OF
∫TRUCTURAL INTEGRITY

HE WAS A SUCCESS. By every standard but money in the bank, Frank Lloyd Wright was a star.

Handsome, clever, quotable, always well dressed, just this side of eccentric, but socially prominent in Chicago circles, he was a public figure regularly seen in newspapers.

A widely known lecturer on many subjects—architecture, social reform, cultural change, contemporary artistic movements—he was asked to address organizations, churches, and universities.

After two visits to Japan (on borrowed money) and concentrated study, he had become an expert on Japanese art prints and a respected dealer in Japanese art. He was assembling an extraordinary collection of prints by Japanese masters.

He was one of the most famous architects in America. He had the interest and, largely, the respect of most of the great architects of his day and was receiving more international interest, especially from Germany. His designs for homes were changing the way houses were conceived and constructed. He had dozens of solid commissions for residences and public buildings, and two large commissions completed.

He was a prominent member of the fashionable Oak Park Unitarian congregation, nephew of the famous preacher Jenkin Lloyd Jones, and a friend of Carl Sandburg, Booker T. Washington, politically active Jane Addams of Hull House, and feminist reformer Susan B. Anthony.

At forty-two, he was a father of six and the husband of "Kitty" Wright, the beautiful young mother who had bloomed in her own right as an advocate of early education for children.

Everything was on track.

What went wrong?

Suddenly, without a warning anyone could interpret, Wright threw everything away. In October of 1909 he disappeared. He surfaced in Germany a week later, registered with someone who was *not* Catherine Wright as "Mr. and Mrs. Wright." In an age when public respectability was sacred, certainly essential to business, Wright left his wife, children, home, architectural practice, city, and country to run off with one of his client's wives.

His lover was Mamah (pronounced MAY-*muh*) Cheney, wife of Edwin H. Cheney, an electrical engineer. Wright and Edwin were friends, both keen automobilists. Wright had built the Oak Park Cheney house in mid-1904. Edwin was described as handsome, intelligent, affable, sweet . . . generally a pleasant and inoffensive man.

Mamah was intense, not as sociable as most. She was an intellectual and a follower of the then-radical feminist ideas of Swedish activist Ellen Key. She and Catherine Wright moved in the same Oak Park circles and were acquaintances, though not close friends. She was not the image of a wild woman, a homewrecker, or a siren. Indeed, Catherine Wright was far more attractive.

Why, shocked Oak Park residents asked one another, would Wright throw everything in his life away for Mamah Cheney?

Or did he? Probably not. It's unlikely that Mamah was the cause of Wright's explosive departure, which was as theatrical as a magician's trick: flash, bang, a puff of smoke and he was gone.

As with everything else in Wright's life, only Wright pulled the strings. Wright led Wright astray. Frank Lloyd Wright had plunged into a chasm in his own personality. Whether we call it a breakdown, sudden lunacy, or a mid-life crisis, he exploded the attractive, conventional structure that held him to respectable life in Oak Park, Illinois, in one vicious gesture.

Biographers, critics, and historians have written a lot about this "sudden" change as a flaw in his character. It's true that his character wasn't entirely admirable. He wasn't always a pleasant man, and was seldom accused of being scrupulously truthful. He was a narcissist, obsessed by his own wants and feelings, regardless of others. He demanded flattery and complete attention, and preferred disciples to friends. The long friendships he maintained with powerful men were self-serving; he used his charm and fellowship to manipulate them shamelessly. But none of these self-aggrandizing faults accounts for the harm he did to himself and his reputation.

What was missing in his heart? Was Wright grieving for his father's love? Was he confused by his mother's alternate adoration and harsh criticism? Did he mourn a family he never had? Acceptance? We don't know. If we knew for sure what Frank Lloyd Wright's inner fears were, would they explain his self-destructive behavior? Probably not.

Critics today seize on easy solutions: they suggest this was an expression of his lack of morals. But Wright wasn't a rake or wolf. He always loved being around pretty women, but he basked in the reflected glow of their beauty, almost certainly believing that it showed him in a good light. If anything, he was a bit prudish and old-fashioned about sexual conduct.

Still, the wrecking gesture that separated him from conventional life came from somewhere, and it didn't come as suddenly as it seemed to. It was only a final bloom of angry frustration that had been growing in him for years. His volatile feelings were nurtured by events and situations that don't mean much separately. Together, however, they may give us some idea of what sparked the flash and bang of Frank Lloyd Wright's breakout.

On June 6, 1904, William Wright died at seventy-nine. Frank hadn't seen his father since he had left Anna's house. Robert Llewellyn, Frank's sixth child, was born a few months before, but William had not seen any of them. Frank despised his father for obscure reasons of his own, but now the old man was dead. The death of a father, loved or hated, is a message from fate: death will harvest you, as well.

Yes, it was a time of great success, but at what a heavy price! Wright was keeping up an almost super-human schedule of work and creation. The workload was beginning to tell: his draftsmen noticed that he was overtired, overextended, frayed. The work required hours of intense concentration, study, revisions, draw-ing. When he wasn't at the boards, he was "onstage," selling himself and his services to prospective clients, with all the tension of possible failure.

Improvident, extravagant, he was deeply in debt, borrowing money from anyone he could wheedle, even his own employees. The man had no shame when it came to borrowing without the prospect of prompt—

or even eventual—repayment. But there must have been a price for all the debt, a bitterness. One of his own draftsmen loaned him the money for a trip to Japan, where he bought more prints as he traveled around the country in "native" garb. There, he was welcomed as an artist, connoisseur, and expert. Why was he forced to borrow paltry sums from lesser men to achieve the great things of which he was capable? It must have pained him.

He was creating new, distinct styles of architecture with bold new directions in shaping American homes and business. But new steps bring new criticism. Some architectural commentators called the Larkin Building spectacularly ugly. They found no homey charm in his radical homes. They declared that the Unity Temple looked more like a counting house than a church. Criticism, which came easy to Wright's lips, galled when it was applied to his great work.

Fatherhood was never a joy to Wright. He never had a father feeling for his children. He wanted them kept at a distance, orderly and quiet.

Frank demanded undivided attention. After she had children, his Kitty was no longer exclusively his.

She spent more and more time with the noisy boys and girls, and less with him. She could no longer supply the idol worship he wanted, because Catherine Wright had grown up. She was no longer his adoring child bride. She was a woman at thirty-six, accomplished in her own ways, with her own interests and talents and friends. Catherine's "competing" life of her own felt like a betrayal to a man who needed constant adoration.

At harvest time in 1906, Uncle James Lloyd Jones died. His steam-driven tractor was chuffing from one oat field to another when it crashed through a bridge across a gully, killing two workers. Uncle James struggled to reach the men but caught his leg in the spokes of a wheel, and mangled it badly. He died days later.

An unexpected shock surfaced after his death. James, one of the practical, conservative, steady uncles who had criticized Frank for his wild life and impractical designs, was calamitously in debt for $65,000, an unbelievable sum in 1906. He had borrowed to buy land, adding to his farm holdings in the valley of the Lloyd Joneses, but the value of crops had bottomed out and he was forced to borrow even more. Worse, his brothers and his sisters had been co-signing loans for him. They were now responsible for his debts.

In 1909, a few months before Frank's explosive departure, James's debts forced Aunts Nell and Jane to declare bankruptcy for themselves and their beloved Hillside School.

The family that was Frank's model of strength and solidity, of propriety and comfort, was nearly destroyed by the same monetary demons that hounded him. What chance did he have?

Wright may have believed that his marriage was flawed. He had been unable to design or craft a *perfect* marriage to his specifications. His life as an Oak Park citizen was flawed. He couldn't engineer his social, financial, or professional life to be *perfect*. He had no stomach for rebuilding, remodeling, and repairing. Perhaps that grinding work felt too much like the endless process of paying back all his debts.

It's not up to us to excuse Frank Lloyd Wright for his departure. He abandoned his wife of twenty years and his children, leaving them with the Yellow Devil and a grocery bill of nine hundred dollars. We should try to understand, however, that this irresponsible act was due to some mental breakdown that he couldn't control. Just as he used his rich friends, Wright probably used Mamah Cheney to reject his entire life and begin a new life.

Perhaps he could make this one perfect.

• 9 •

LOSING EDEN

WRIGHT CHOSE GERMANY as his destination
for a reason. His work was closely watched and even
celebrated by young German architects. The German publisher Ernst Wasmuth wanted to produce a
portfolio of his work: *Ausgeführte Bauten und Entwürfe
von Frank Lloyd Wright* (*The Completed Buildings and
Designs of Frank Lloyd Wright*).

Wright saw the Wasmuth portfolio as a multiple
opportunity. It got him away from Chicago. It gave the
unschooled, relatively untraveled architect a chance to
see the ancient and modern architecture of Europe.
It broadened his reputation as an architect. The large
format portfolio, meant for serious collectors, aggrandized Wright as an artist as much as an architect and

put him in the same class as his beloved printmakers Hokusai and Hiroshige. Marketed shrewdly to wealthy collectors, the portfolio could be profitable.

For this last reason, Wright arranged to buy out the entire printing.

To help him with the work of making the drawings, he summoned two young helpers: his eighteen-year-old son Frank Lloyd Wright, Jr. (known as Lloyd), and draftsman Taylor Woolley. When Lloyd arrived, he found his father had shifted his ground and was happily housed in Villino Fortuna, a not-so-small villa in Fiesole, Italy.

Why did Catherine Wright allow Lloyd to join his father? She was a remarkably placid, mature woman who believed for many years that Frank would return to her. His departure, painful as it must have been, seemed to her a storm that would pass.

Wright loved Italy. Fiesole was just outside Florence, Michelangelo's city. The villas in those hills, built for medieval and renaissance noblemen, fascinated him. They were tiny, self-contained kingdoms with their own workshops, barns, vineyards, fields, banqueting halls, and stables. Their old, honest shapes and earthy colors seemed like part of the sunny slopes.

He and the boys worked on the portfolio in a daze of happiness with Italy, the drawings, and prospects for the future. Mamah translated the poetry of Goethe and Swedish works by Ellen Key about sexual freedom and female equality.

Some of Key's philosophy crept into Wright's way of justifying his offenses against society, Catherine, and his family. He began to refer to marriage as "marital slavery." Perhaps he identified too much with the Italian Renaissance princes; he proclaimed that the artist was a higher form of humanity, and thereby above the social rules and restraints of common men. He began to engineer a plan.

Wright's abandonment of Catherine and six children was probably some episode of desperate madness, but the cold-blooded, self-serving, manipulative plan he later carried out with relentless timing is harder to overlook.

In the summer of 1910, when the Wasmuth portfolio was well under way, Frank Lloyd Wright returned to Catherine and Oak Park. But not as a repentant husband. He arrived on the attack, accusing Catherine. Perhaps he would come back, but he had a list of demands for more freedom, more respect, more attention to his needs. It was Catherine who was guilty—of neglect: she hadn't supported him as an artist and creator should be, *must* be supported! And he didn't come back all the way. He didn't live at his Oak Park home but at an apartment in Chicago.

The children were confused. Catherine was gracious and calm. Frank played an elegantly conceived role as a defiant nobleman, a genius battered by middle-class morality.

What about Mamah? He claimed that he left her in Europe because their holy romance would be cheapened by day-to-day living. With reasoning like this, he may have been as confused as the children.

But his plan was afoot. Mamah was to stay in Europe until her divorce from Edwin was final in the summer of 1911. Wright would be busy remodeling the Oak Park studio as a residence for Catherine so the main house could be rented out to provide income for her. His mother, Anna, had her nearby home on the market and was quietly buying up property in Spring Green, in the Lloyd Jones valley of Wisconsin, a few hours away by train.

Wright repented only to those who might help him, especially W. E. and D. D. Martin. To them he claimed deep shame and distress over his wicked conduct. And, by the way, would D. D. kindly help his mother out of a jam? She had bought property in Spring Green so she could return to her home, but her house hadn't sold yet. Might he advance her a bit to buy the new place? D. D., always helpful, always gullible, took over Anna's mortgage in Oak Park.

Within the year, using money freed up when D. D. Martin took over Anna's mortgage, Wright began to build a princely compound on the shoulder of a hill in Spring Green. It was his fantastic version of an Italian nobleman's villa, designed expansively to embrace its own shops, studios, stables, homes, vineyards, lakes, pools, and everything else that could make it self-sustainable. It was to be a fortress of beauty and sense against the gross world beyond the hills. Soaked in his own grandiose melodrama, he called it Taliesin.

The name comes from a Welsh myth. A magical boy endured great suffering and grew into the poet-wizard *Taliesin*—in Welsh, "shining brow," for his broad, bright forehead.

The name supposedly refers to the bright shape of the new architecture just beneath the brow of the Spring Green hill, a "shining brow." But we can assume Wright saw himself as the sorcerer/poet demigod.

He threw himself into the design and construction of his Wisconsin villa with more manic energy than he had ever spent. He called in dozens of masons, carpenters, landscape gardeners, and took on new assistants to help him with Taliesin and with the outside commissions he had left.

Wright in his Wisconsin kingdom, Taliesin.

In the autumn of 1911, when her divorce was final, Mamah Cheney moved into Taliesin. Wright gave up all pretext of returning to Catherine, all expressions of repentance. He took a strange delight in his reputation as a scoundrel and immoral artist.

Modern journalism's *paparazzi* and tabloids are pale and sedate beside the muck-raking newspapers of the early twentieth century. Hard-news reporters drilled for juicy quotes and made up what they couldn't find. A few hours from Chicago they found a love nest, with a society scandal reeking of adulterous sex, Swedish free-love feminism, a wronged wife, and philandering husband, children on both sides without proper homes . . . it was lovely stuff.

Newspapers were primed to believe architects were racy subjects: only a few years before, in 1906, the erratic millionaire Harry K. Thaw had murdered architect Stanford White at White's Madison Square Gardens during a performance of the song "I Could Love a Million Girls." Thaw was jealous that his wife, showgirl Evelyn K. Nesbit, had been a favorite of White's.

It's common to think that Frank Lloyd Wright was

a masterful manipulator of the press. In fact, he did himself great harm by trying to use reporters to deliver his explanations and sermons. He was too vulnerable. It was too easy to show Wright as a windbag and libertine. The strangely righteous, stilted tone of his statements cemented the image of an unrealistic elitist (which, of course, he was).

Wright could be proud, but society could punish. The scandal was damaging. Former Oak Park friends had no interest in his company. Newspapers hounded him for any bit of scandalous news. His business suffered. In 1909 he had ten commissions under design or construction. In 1910, only five. In 1911, just eight. And between 1912 and 1913, Wright had only three commissions. From the most promising and productive architect in the country, Wright had become a social and business pariah.

Wright's troubles were harming his aunts' efforts to reestablish their beloved Hillside School. Fewer respectable people sent their children, because the school had been designed by that wicked architect who left his fine wife, and the infamous love nest was a short walk from the school.

There is a mystery in the published history of

Frank Lloyd Wright during this time. No money was coming in, but Wright was building the most elaborate villa in the Midwest, employing several dozen skilled workmen and using tons of building material. Where did the money come from? No one knows. He had wheedled money out of D. D. Martin and other clients, but these relatively small sums were on another scale. Anna had no money, the aunts were bankrupt, and the Lloyd Jones clan had little but land. Somehow Wright floated the entire project without visible means of support, earning him a place as one of the most talented confidence tricksters in American history.

There is another puzzle, as well. Whatever problems of mind and soul he had run from were left in the Atlantic Ocean. Frank Lloyd Wright was blissfully happy. He was back in high form, creating at a new level. He had passed through the Arts and Crafts Movement, established the Prairie School, and toyed with the International Style, and now he was combining influences from everywhere to synthesize a style that could only be described as *Wrightian.*

His happiness was mirrored in Mamah Cheney's deep, infectious laugh and in the way she was charming the Spring Green neighbors. And happiness seemed justified by the looming prospect of a large commission.

Midway Gardens was a concept that combined elements of the White City and of European beer gardens. Beer gardens were popular in Europe and the United States as family places for dining, singing, dancing, shows, and fun. Wright wanted this commission badly, to try new materials and adapt new influences. Like the Columbian Exposition, it was to be built on the shores of Lake Michigan. He wanted to create a union of all the arts in Midway—architecture, sculpture, mural painting, music, dancing, cuisine—everything. In the summer of 1914, Wright began work on the plans for Midway Gardens. Life was blooming for the revived architect.

John and Lloyd Wright had joined their father's studio and threw themselves into the many layers of design for Midway Gardens. Everything from masonry block to napkins, from plates to murals, from chairs to symbolic sculpture was to be designed in detail by the master. The scale was impressive: the gardens would occupy an entire city block, about two hundred yards on each side. Within its plan, Wright departed from rectangular order and experimented with unusual angles and clever manipulations of level.

In some sense it was a maze, making the site seem much larger than it was. This was one of Wright's best magic tricks, played over and over in all his work. But the visual clues and the graphic themes of sculpture and decoration made navigation through the maze— from concert space to winter garden to restaurant to beer hall to mysterious nooks and vistas—simple and delightful. Wright used Alfonso Iannelli, a familiar collaborator, as the sculptor for the "nymphs" that guarded entrances and visually cued visitors.

The style that was buzzing in Wright's welcoming mind at the time was essentially American but ancient. In the mid–nineteenth century, the lost civilizations of the Maya, Aztec, Inca, and Olmec were rediscovered in Mexico and Central America. In the 1890s, a British explorer brought out the first photographs of the ruins and an early catalogue of Mayan structures. In 1911, American explorer Hiram Bingham rediscovered the mysterious Incan city of Machu Picchu in the Andes. In 1915 there was an influential show of Mayan artifacts and photos in Los Angeles. These ancient works spoke to Wright's existing fascination with American Indian themes and decoration. The rhythmically textured masonry of the Mayan façades crept into Wright's work. He loved the raised patterns and complex frieze of window openings. Mayan influence is obvious in the design of Midway Gardens. Even Iannelli's nymphs bear some resemblance to the giant Olmec faces and the Mayan pottery gods.

Midway Gardens was a big commission and a whirlpool of demanding work, tugging Wright away from his beautiful Taliesin during the summer of 1914. And who could blame him for hating to leave that magical place?

It's difficult to overlook Frank Lloyd Wright's self-delusions and egotistical grandstanding. But if we can put those aside, we see that his creation of Taliesin gave all of us a gift of exquisite beauty and a model for architecture that will still be inspiring designers and even common homeowners for another hundred years, at least. Taliesin, in all the forms it would take over the years, was a masterwork of immense understanding. The whole, the parts, the details, the site, the flow of space—everything fits and delights. Every line and detail of Taliesin demonstrates Wright's dazzling ability to create comforting, encouraging, sheltering, inspiring space for human beings.

Wright made pompous claims of being super-human, beyond simple citizens. Yet that's not what the architecture of Taliesin tells us. The flamboyant rogue tells us, "You'll never understand my genius." But Taliesin tells us, "Sit down, make yourself at home." His extraordinary genius was in building for ordinary people. He was better at that than anyone had ever been. Did he really believe that he was the poet-sorcerer Taliesin? We could almost believe him if we didn't see the human flaws, and if we didn't see the terrible price he would pay.

August 15, 1914, was warm and pleasant in the hills of Wisconsin. Frank, John, and Lloyd were working on drawings for Midway Gardens at their office in Orchestra Hall, in Chicago. Wright's sister Jennie and her husband Andrew Porter were summering at the little house Wright had designed for them in the Lloyd Jones valley near Taliesin.

Mamah was at Taliesin, visited by her two children, Martha, almost nine, and John, twelve. Six of Wright's workmen and draftsmen were having lunch in a room off Taliesin's kitchen. The only other person at Taliesin was Julian Carlton. His wife, Gertrude, was running an errand. They were both black servants.

There had been some trouble with Julian, a trim, intelligent man from Barbados. Proud and nervous, he had objected to the demeaning way in which he was treated by the white workmen. It would be half a century before there was substantial Civil Rights progress in the United States. In 1914 the place of African Americans in white society was uncomfortable. Julian hadn't shown the proper meek attitude, so he and his wife had been told to find another job at the end of the week.

In his white serving coat, Julian quietly laid out lunch for the six workmen and left. He closed the door behind him. He locked the door.

A few moments later, liquid came gushing in under the locked door and the men smelled gasoline. It burst into flames, trapping them. Herbert Fritz realized his clothes were on fire. He leaped through a window, breaking his arm, and rolled down the hill to put out the flames. The other men leaped out after him, but one by one Julian struck their heads with a hatchet. Thomas Bruckner, Emil Brodelle, and Ernest

Weston, thirteen, were killed within a few moments. Billy Weston, Ernest's father, and David Lindblom were only stunned.

At some point Julian walked out onto the terrace where Mamah and her children were lunching. He killed all three with the hatchet. He soaked their bodies with gasoline and set them burning.

Though badly burned, Lindblom ran half a mile with Weston to get help.

Six people were dead, and beautiful Taliesin was in flames. When Billy Weston returned, he dragged out the fire hose and fought the flames until he collapsed. When help from Spring Green arrived, Lindblom collapsed. He would later die from his burns. Only Herbert Fritz, a draftsman, and Billy Weston, Wright's master carpenter, survived the cataclysm. And only a small part of Taliesin was saved from the fire.

Someone called Wright's office. John and Lloyd gently took their dazed father to the train station. Standing on the platform, waiting for the same train, Edwin Cheney walked to Wright and took his hands. They shared their grief and a compartment for the ride to Spring Green.

The next day Julian Carlton was discovered

hiding in the unlit firebox of the Taliesin furnace. He had tried to commit suicide by drinking acid but had only succeeded in burning his mouth and throat beyond speech. Spring Green citizens made some moves to lynch Carlton (a common fate for accused black men at the time), but the sheriff fought them off and jailed him for trial. He never reached trial and was never able to speak his reasons for the killing spree. Refusing to eat, he died within the month.

On August 16, 1914, Edwin Cheney departed from Spring Green with a single coffin bearing the burned bodies of his children. He left Mamah's body with Wright.

A plain pine box was built and filled with flowers from Mamah's garden. Her body was placed inside and the lid nailed home. More flowers were in the horse-drawn wagon. The whole garden was cut down so that the dug grave was filled with flowers, flowers, flowers. The box was lowered into them. It began to rain. Wright asked the others to leave and took up the spade to fill in the grave by himself.

• 10 •

THE VAMP

THE DESTRUCTION OF Taliesin was almost complete.

After such a cataclysm we might expect Wright's life to be a burnt shell as well. But he wasn't destroyed. There was a brief period of confusion and depression, but Wright's buoyant spirit burst out of the depths. His tragedy, as grisly and somber as some Greek play, seemed to energize him. In a few weeks he had summoned even more workmen and assistants to rebuild Taliesin on the same lines.

Wait, not exactly the same! He saw improvements, new possibilities. His mind was racing.

Do artists differ from normal people? Is creativity a kind of insanity? All of us are capable of art and creativity, and we aren't all insane, but what about the great artists? Some live unremarkable lives but do remarkable work. Away from his easel, Rembrandt van Rijn was an unimpressive family man. Some artists seem strange only because their fame invites us to look closely at their lives. Most lives have strange details. True, some great artists have been famous for their wild lifestyles, antics, relationships, and bizarre behavior. Great artists may simply have more enthusiasm and drive than normal people. They want or need to say more, show more, do more, prove more. And this largeness is necessary, because creation is a chancy, disappointing business. For every masterpiece on an artist's drawing board, dozens of un-masterpieces are shoved into the wastebasket. Great art is necessarily public (or it wouldn't be famous), and the public is not predictable. To deal with the public, the artist must have the buoyancy to deal with the frustration of being criticized, unrewarded, or prevented from continuing. There are thousands of uncompleted masterpieces of art and architecture, dozens of them Wright's. So that enthusiasm, that largeness of spirit some see as insanity, may be necessary to go on with the work. And on, and on, after many disappointments.

Wright's enthusiastic spirit was large enough to bounce back and go on.

The reborn villa, Taliesin II, was buzzing like a beehive. Wright's sister Jennie ran the kitchen, feeding at least two dozen every day. The Lloyd Jones clan gathered their support around Frank. The buildings and grounds grew beyond the original scope. It was now planned to embrace not only a residence for Wright, himself, but also homes for Anna (seldom far from Frank), Aunts Nell and Jane, Wright's draftsmen and their wives, servants, gardeners, mechanics, carpenters, and horses.

The Taliesin stables housed horses for farmwork, hauling, and pleasure. The rolling Wisconsin countryside in 1915 offered fine riding, and Wright was a masterful horseman. He rode blooded stock, wore tailored riding breeches, and ordered custom saddlery, as befitted a prince in the country.

D. D. Martin's frequent advice to economize, scale back, be realistic, live within a budget, was merrily ignored. Wright was hell-bent on overcoming the tragedy of Mamah's murder, and he rolled everything else into the category of distractions to be trodden down—

criticism, creditors, interference of any kind. Against all financial restraint, he ordered new grand pianos.

World War I had begun. It was, to Wright, a European affair and not an American concern. He was politically unsophisticated, even illogical, and saw the brutal slaughter as a British error. (His Welsh rebel mindset usually cast England as the villain.) German architects had always been kind to him, hadn't they? Wright and Uncle Jenkin Jones were loudly against American involvement. Both insisted it was best to ignore the war entirely and let those people across the sea do whatever they wished. Wright continued to expand Taliesin II and complete Midway Gardens.

We've seen how vulnerable wealthy clients were to Wright's charm and flattery. But he himself could be woefully susceptible to manipulation. It was Wright's vulnerability to flattery and drama that snared him into another romantic misadventure.

The studio mail was heavy with letters of sympathy from all over the world. Wright's assistants screened the mail efficiently, holding most of the bills and passing on only "important" business letters, notes from close friends, and a few exceptional consolations.

One fateful letter that was put into his hands came from a self-proclaimed sculptress, a young widow who had been living in Paris until the war, Maude Miriam Noel.

Her letter was perfumed with praise for his greatness. His depth of soul and creative power, she suggested, made his grief even deeper and more profound than ordinary mortals could suffer. She, too, had known grief. Only those of true artistic temperament (a group in which she included herself without actually mentioning it) could know true sadness. She wished him well and signed herself "Madame Noel."

It is difficult to write about Miriam Noel without making her sound like a cartoon. Her speech and writing were impossibly flowery, even by the standards of her day. She traveled with trunks of clothes and had a strange fashion sense: one of her outfits might include a turban, cape, necklaces, chokers, bracelets, rings, sashes, and a monocle hung from a ribbon. In her mid-forties, she was the widow of a department-store businessman, accustomed to some wealth, and was an accomplished social climber. She had a Southern accent and a mysterious, dramatic manner. Part of the mystery was certainly her enormous store of romantic illusions. She was a Christian Scientist, believed in ghosts and spirit mediums, attended séances, and was convinced that she could read others' thoughts and even the future. She was also convinced that her fate was to be part of a mythic love-bond with a famous artistic superman. Frank fit the fantasy.

Her photos aren't impressive. It's possible that she was beautiful in the way photographs don't show. There must have been something powerfully compelling about her. Occasionally, very intelligent people live with a hidden mental illness that translates into a peculiar glitter, like an attractive flame. Miriam Noel's flame was fatally beautiful to Frank Lloyd Wright when he met her. She set her charm and her mysterious glitter to snare him. To use a word from her time, she was a vamp.

A few days after their meeting, she was addressing passionate letters to him as "lord of my waking dreams." In a few weeks she had moved into his Chicago apartment with him.

Miriam was an expert flatterer. She was also an unstable and thorny personality. Wright and Miriam began to argue almost immediately, probably whenever he didn't choose to mold himself to her romantic illusions. She was also hotly jealous, accusing him of flirting with young women. He probably did, but he flirted with *everyone*.

Miriam moved in, she moved out, she moved in. She left for Albuquerque. She returned. To casual acquaintances and business friends they were a handsome couple. But at close quarters they were a stormy, surly pair. The turmoil wore down Wright's close friends and employees. Yet the frenzied melodrama in their quarrels appealed to both of them. High drama was something they needed.

By the summer of 1915 she was installed at Taliesin II, and the situation took a stranger turn.

Wright had hired an older housekeeper at Taliesin II, Nellie Breen. She was cranky and disapproved strongly of Madame Noel, so she lost her job. Before she left, however, Breen intercepted several letters sent by Miriam to Wright during one of the times she had flounced away. They were wildly emotional, accusing him in gaudy language of cruelty, mental torture, and other inflated rantings. Breen sold these letters to the newspapers, still busily digging up dirt on the libertine architect.

Not satisfied with this indignity, Breen took herself down to the Department of Justice. A few years before, in an attempt to stop widespread prostitution, the Mann Act had been established, prohibiting the transport of a woman across state lines for immoral purposes. Breen gave evidence that placed Wright and Miriam in his Chicago apartment, and then placed them in Wisconsin at Taliesin II. He had taken her across the state line, they weren't married, and they were sleeping together. Wright was charged under the Mann Act. The newspapers were deliriously happy.

Even Wright, who affected a distance from sordid legal details, knew that a federal charge was serious business. He hired a friend, perhaps the greatest trial lawyer of the early twentieth century, Clarence Darrow, who would later become famous for, among other things, the Scopes "Monkey Trial," defending the right of a biology teacher to teach evolution in Tennessee. Darrow looked closely at the case and had it dismissed, using the fact that Breen had sent threatening letters to Miriam and was, therefore, an unreliable witness. Wright must have sighed mightily when the Justice Department was no longer after him, but it wouldn't be the last time. And it wouldn't be the last time Wright would provide racy stories for the tabloids.

Bit by bit, it would become clear that Miriam was a deeply troubled woman and addicted to morphine. She was unpredictable and dangerous. Wright would later discover that she had been arrested by the Paris police for trying to kill a former lover.

Now Wright had two crazy women in his life— Anna Wright and Miriam. Worse, Anna hated Miriam Noel.

By 1919, it was time for Wright to make another getaway, and the Japanese emperor provided one.

• 11 •

RING OF FIRE

ACROSS THE WORLD, the court of the emperor of Japan and the city of Tokyo needed a large hotel in the European style.

A decaying, damp German hotel built in the 1870s served European and American visitors. Japan had been open to foreign view for only about sixty years, since Commodore Perry's visit and treaty with the emperor in 1854. For over two hundred years before that, Japan had been closed to foreign visitors. Now the imperial court wished to house and entertain foreigners in a way that reflected Japan's wealth and new industrial might. Twelve years before Wright arrived in the spring of 1919, the Japanese battle fleet had annihilated the Russian Imperial fleet at the Battle of

Tsushima. Mighty salvos from Admiral Togo's guns announced a new era for warfare and for Japan. The Land of the Rising Sun would greet its Western guests as a modern world power.

Baron Okura of the court of the Japanese emperor had approached Frank Lloyd Wright. In January of 1913, Frank and Mamah had spent six months in Japan to win the commission.

Wright was chosen from among all the architects of America and Europe because of his ability to bring nature into architecture. The essential heart of Japan was reverence for the natural world. The love of wood and stone and handwork, so pleasing to the Arts and Crafts Movement, had always been a passion in Japanese building. Homes were made of wood, stone, paper, and tile left largely in their natural state. Structural elements like beams and pillars weren't hidden but expressed honestly. Floor plans were open and flexible. Rooms could be changed in a few moments by rearranging light wood and paper *shoji* screens. There was a strong connection between the inner house and garden spaces around it; they were both part of the living environment. The parallels to Wright's work were unmistakable.

Wright was enchanted by Japanese architecture and by the natural mythology of the Japanese: for them, even mute stones, winds, and trees had distinct identities. Curiously, he made no effort to incorporate Japanese themes into his design for the hotel. It was to be all-Wright, and all-American. Central American, in fact. Wright's knowledge of Mayan architecture heavily influenced the design for the new Imperial Hotel.

Wright and Miriam arrived in Tokyo in the spring of 1919. They were treated like royalty. Wright was addressed with the honorific "Wright-san" and furnished with a multi-room suite in the old German hotel, a car, and a chauffeur. As always, he created an elaborate workspace before he began the work.

There was a serious structural hurdle to building in Tokyo. The city was founded on eight feet of topsoil over sixty feet of river mud, and it stood directly on the Ring of Fire.

Tectonically, the seabed of the Pacific Ocean is an enormous series of plates of rock expanding east and west from spreading centers in the deep ocean. The gargantuan pressure of the heavy ocean plates sliding under the less dense land plates near the shores causes friction and heat. The heat creates sometimes explosive risings of molten rock; we call them volcanoes. Land plates shift along the expanding edge, slipping with a shock we know as an earthquake. The resulting areas of seismic activity and active volcanoes around the Pacific plate are called the Ring of Fire. On the western side of the Ring, Japan has a history of frequent and disastrous earthquakes that have destroyed whole cities. Wright knew that when an earthquake struck Tokyo, its mud would shimmy like a bowl of jelly, destroying any rigid thing on it. How could he prevent destruction?

At Adler and Sullivan, Wright had become acquainted with an accomplishment of Sullivan's former boss, William Le Baron Jenney. A fine engineer, Jenney had invented a foundation that could support the weight of a stone and brick building on the poor silt soil of Chicago. Wright and his *lieber Meister* had used Jenney's solution many times: a "floating" foundation made of driven piles beneath a stable, steel-reinforced concrete pad.

Wright had also learned something from the windmill tower he built for his aunts: the oak tree's strength wasn't in its rigidity but in its ability to flex with the wind and let the blast pass.

He conceived his own version of the floating foundation: concrete "finger piles" driven into loose topsoil under steel-reinforced concrete "ground beams" linked to one another by notches. Wright knew that an earthquake's shocks came in waves. He reasoned that as they passed under the pads, the finger piles would flex. He segmented the larger structure of the hotel to rest on individual pads. Segments were connected to one another by slots and pins that would ride the earthquake's waves without tearing away.

He made the walls wider at the base, keeping their center of gravity low so they were unlikely to topple. He knew that an earthquake could send the traditional Japanese roof tiles flying like bullets, so he designed a flexible copper roof weathered to a soft, natural green. He laid the delicate electric, plumbing, and gas lines in shallow concrete trays trenched around the building. The greatest hazard of an earthquake was a fire afterward, so he designed ponds and reflecting pools to store firefighting water nearby. It was an impressive demonstration of engineering details.

The design of the Imperial Hotel is unmistakably Wright, yet it stands outside the path of his Ameri-

can designs. Looking at the Imperial beside the greater body of his work is puzzling—as if a pianist in the
middle of a show tune broke into a funeral dirge, then
returned to happy music. There were grand things in
the design, but it doesn't fit Wright's other work. It was
dark, heavy, cavelike, and formal.

Some critics see his grief for Mamah and his strife
with Miriam in the somber style of the Imperial.
Doubtful. Architecture doesn't reflect mood like music
or painting, and Wright didn't react to grief like most
men. He wasn't that sensitive. He did some of his light-
est, most playful work at dark times.

Two reasons are more likely.

One is that the elaborately polite and formal Japanese, with all their bowing and honorifics, led the old
rogue to believe a bit too much in his own pretentious
image. He was thrilled to have an army of six hundred
master craftsmen working under his orders. He must
have felt like a pharaoh building a pyramid, more like
a holy man than an architect.

Another cause could be his fee. With large buildings, the fee of the architect is a percentage of the
building's price. Wright designed, redesigned, over

designed, and revised constantly. The costlier the building, the more Wright got paid. No one knows for sure what the complete cost was, or his fee. The best estimates are that he drove the price up to $4.5 million, and that his fee, gauged by normal standards, would have been close to $500,000. This was in 1920 dollars, a sum that would be many millions today.

In the Imperial Hotel, Wright continued to explore his Mayan theme, with its friezes of repeated deep-relief stonework and carving details. Each guest room was different, with clever lighting and built-in furniture. The mood of the Imperial was heavy, monumental, formal, and gave an overwhelming impression of mass pressing down on the earth. In the courtyard or at the registration desk of the Imperial Hotel, a Mayan human sacrifice wouldn't be out of character. The imperial court loved it.

Between 1919 and 1922 Wright spent part of each year in Japan. It was a suspended time in Wright's life. Miriam lived with him in their luxurious suite, and they were driven about the city by the chauffeur. The daily press of the project's multitude of design challenges and the exotic setting may have provided enough drama to quiet their own dramatic battles.

The Japanese-Mayan Imperial Hotel in Tokyo.

Wright indulged himself in some spectacularly strange costumes, complete with pith helmets, high-heeled boots, puff-bottom trousers, and oversized silk bow ties.

In all his time in Japan, he never learned more than a few words of Japanese. He directed his workmen through a Japanese assistant, architect Arato Endo. He loved Japanese art and made frequent collecting trips, buying an unbelievable two freight cars full of

Japanese prints and art treasures. He expended a great part of his fee on art. And yet he didn't love the society of Japan: it was totalitarian, demanding compliance in dress, custom, and thought from each of its citizens. Though Japan revered Wright as an artist, foreigners were considered barbarians. It was a self-centered society that held anything outside its strict "normality" in poor regard. He realized that he could never thrive or even exist in such a narrow culture. Though he was loud in his criticism of American culture, it was forgiving and even encouraging to eccentric geniuses.

The relationship between Miriam and Wright was wearing down. Her interludes of strange behavior upset him, and their stormy partnership drained his energy. One of her fits of strange feeling paid off, however. She had a sense of foreboding on an afternoon when they were to attend a garden party. She refused to go, staying behind at the old German Imperial Hotel. The hotel burned.

Fire followed Wright throughout his life like a pursuing demon.

What good luck that Miriam was in their suite! She threw $40,000 of prints and other art treasures out their window to the chauffeur below. Was Miriam prescient? Could she sense the future? No, Wright simply didn't record the other times she had feelings of dread and nothing happened. Luck was with them, not paranormal powers.

The fire brought more pressure to bear on building the new Imperial Hotel. Tokyo was now without large rooms for balls, receptions, and dinners. Within six weeks, Wright produced designs for a new reception wing. This was a trick he called "shaking a design out of my sleeve."

After years of traveling back and forth across the Pacific (Wright was a terrible sailor and was seasick most of the time), increasing pressure to finish the Imperial, and growing dissatisfaction from his imperial clients, Wright was dangerously stressed. He collapsed with serious pneumonia. Mother Anna, at eighty-one, rushed to her boy's side. It was a showy but useless effort, since Anna immediately came down with dysentery and was in bed for weeks.

By 1922, Baron Okura and the financial backers were furious. Wright had stubbornly exceeded the building budget and delayed the schedule at every turn. He was about to be fired. But on April 26, 1922, a fierce earthquake struck Tokyo. The ruins of the old German Imperial came crashing down, but the new Imperial stood safely. This event allowed both sides to part on pleasant terms. Wright left three months later after completing the drawings for the new wing.

Wright's Imperial Hotel opened formally on September 1, 1923. At 11:58 that morning, Tokyo was struck by the Great Kanto Earthquake, the most severe shock ever recorded in Japan, estimated at 7.8 to 8.4 on the Richter scale. Most of the city was destroyed. Fires swept uncontrollably through the wood-and-paper buildings of Tokyo and Yokohama. As many as 140,000 people may have been killed.

Wright received the first news of the quake at his new office in Los Angeles: the Imperial Hotel had been destroyed. Sweeter word arrived two days later. The Imperial Hotel was not destroyed. It survived the quake with only minor damage and became a center for the injured and for refugees, and temporary headquarters for the embassies of several nations. The charming pools on which Wright had insisted were, indeed, used for fighting nearby fires.

In his *Autobiography* the survival of the hotel is

inflated to heroic proportions. Wright even includes a telegram from Baron Okura praising the miraculous building as "a monument to your genius."

Did the Wright finger-floating foundation work? Yes and no.

What the *Autobiography* doesn't mention is that the Imperial wasn't the only survivor: *all* modern steel-reinforced buildings in Tokyo withstood the Kanto Earthquake. No copy of Baron Okura's original telegram has been found; it's possible that Wright wrote the telegram himself. Still, Wright had fulfilled his contract in a workmanlike way: to design a showplace structure that would withstand seismic stresses. He deserves much credit for that.

The Imperial Hotel was demolished in 1968. The hotel was no longer considered a first-class destination, and the floating foundation had allowed parts of the heavy masonry structure to sink into the soft earth as much as four feet. Restoring the rooms to contemporary standards and repairing the foundation would have been too expensive.

The complex, dark, but impressive lobby of the Imperial Hotel was carefully dismantled and reconstructed in Nagoya as a permanent exhibit.

The enshrined lobby of the Imperial Hotel is one design icon from this project, but there is another. When John Lloyd Wright came to Japan to help his father with working drawings, he was impressed with the way concrete beams in the floating foundations were notched into one another to form a stable structure. When he returned to the United States, he invented and manufactured a child's building set of notched hardwood dowels that locked together like the foundation. Millions were made, and they're still made today: Lincoln Logs.

• 12 •

HOLLYWOOD DRAMA

LOS ANGELES BECAME a stopover as Wright went to and from Japan. His son Lloyd had established an office there and was doing well as a designer at the new Paramount Studios. His success and the sunny optimism of the southern California weather plucked at Wright's attention. There was also a building boom in California. For a few years Papa Wright had a half-hearted notion that he would set up shop on the West Coast.

He always believed that he could master any new landscape or situation, and the challenge of a new billboard on which to write his name large was seductive. Wright, more than most architects, accepted commissions for which he simply had no time. He counted on his reputation and the client's patience to smooth over the schedule difficulties.

In 1914 he was asked to design an artist's colony on a thirty-six-acre plot of ground in the (then) sleepy little village of Los Angeles. His client, Aline Barnsdall, wasn't swept away by Wright's charm. She was in every way Wright's equal—tough, intellectual, demanding, and bubbling over with ideas. Between 1914 and 1924 she commissioned forty-five projects from Wright, and for a good part of that time they were at each other's throats, arguing and accusing. Most of the forty-five commissions were never built. The uncomfortable relationship between the wealthy, independent woman and the flamboyant, autocratic architect produced only one large and decidedly un-cozy house, two satellite guest houses, and a kindergarten.

Hollyhock House was named after Barnsdall's favorite flower, which is represented in masonry and art-glass details all over the house. The stark, sprawling, over-formal house is another grim Mayan temple. It isn't Wright's best work, but it reveals his genius for responding to the local cues of nature. Wisconsin is a lush, green, growing climate. Southern Calfornia is dry and blond, parched by a daily, unblinking sun on rocky young mountains. It's possible that Wright associated the harsh climate with the harsh character of Mayan civilization. Hollyhock House looks more like a fortress, but it isn't solid or honest. What looks like unyielding stone is really stucco over wood framing. It doesn't suggest anything of warmth or family.

But its intricate decorations and rhythmic details have made Hollyhock House one of America's registered architectural treasures.

Most owners of Wright homes want to live in them forever, leaks and all. Aline Barnsdall moved out after three years and gave the entire property to the City of Los Angeles.

Local interest in the Barnsdall projects brought Wright commissions for four new houses. Wright used all of his houses as laboratories, and these California houses were a set of exciting experiments. As with most early experiments, problems in theory surfaced, but better solutions followed.

Over two thousand years ago, Roman engineers discovered a miracle material: concrete. It's a two-part material: cement (which hardens during a chemical reaction with water) and aggregate (sand and small stones that give the cement body). Roman cement occurred in natural deposits called *pozzolana*, a mix of clay and limestone heated to high temperatures by the volcano, Mount Vesuvius, and named after the nearby town of Pozzuoli. Modern cement is manufactured by baking crushed limestone with clay. It's mixed with water and sand at the site or on the way to a building site in a cement-mixer truck, then poured into molds for foundations or walls. At the cement factory it's also molded into the humble gray, useful concrete block we all recognize.

Wright was fascinated by concrete, perhaps because mixing it with local sand and stones made a house part of the earth around it. He saw it as pourable, moldable stone. Most architects used it as a dreary filler, something to be hidden by surface treatments. Wright recognized concrete's potential and played with it, invented with it, stretched its limits. He believed it could be both the structure and the outer garment of great houses.

While supervising the weaving of custom rugs in Beijing, Wright's attention had fallen on the strong matrix of heavy fiber that held the colorful and textural tufts of yarn in place. Wright was always responsive to the merest breeze of suggestion. He began to think of a structural system using cheap concrete modules within a strong matrix.

Building materials have strengths and weaknesses. Pull a bar of concrete from the ends, and it has very little strength. Push the ends together, and it is strong. The trick is to use a material in the way it *wants* to be used, and to maximize its strengths. Wright knew that the shape of a material is as important as its basic properties: a sheet of thin steel is floppy, but a sheet of corrugated steel of the same thickness is stiff. If he could mold concrete with a deeply "corrugated" face— shaped with deep details—it would be stronger.

The fascination with concrete and with other inexpensive, quick, flexible materials might be an echo of Wright's pleasure at seeing the White City rise so quickly using the wood and fabric staff method. He was constantly searching for newer, simpler, cheaper building materials and methods, and he was always wary of the ways building methods dictated the shape or texture or limits of architecture.

His first house using his "textile block" system was a tiny home and shop for Alice Millard in 1923. As a widow, Alice needed a small home that would protect and showcase her book and antique collections. Alice had bought a typical suburban lot in Los Angeles but when Wright came to inspect it, he was charmed by the nearby arroyo, a dry ravine. He counseled her to give up the flat parcel of land and buy the ravine.

He designed wooden molds for square concrete blocks, using a symmetrical pattern around a cross. Several molds turned out about a hundred blocks a day. Some molds produced pierced blocks—the central cross was empty. Some molds produced plain-faced interior blocks. All blocks were set in mortar with a strip of steel mesh laid into each horizontal mortar joint for strength. The house needed strength: Los Angeles is on the eastern side of the Ring of Fire and subject to earthquakes like Tokyo's.

The repeated pattern of the exterior walls is strikingly beautiful and orderly. Some of the blocks had glass inserts, some formed exterior sun screens. The brilliant California sun changes the look of the block as it changes its angle through the day, and it casts delightful cross patterns on the floor of polished colored concrete. The Mayan theme was still in Wright's thoughts—strong patterns, square design, and flat roofs. It is a jewel. Indeed, Wright named it "La Miniatura" for its small size. Few houses of any size are as pleasant or livable, and it was a favorite of Wright's, who said, "I would rather have built this house than St. Peter's in Rome."

It was a gem but it was nearly lost. Wright was unfamiliar with the nature of arroyos. They are dry throughout the year except during rare cloudbursts, when they can be choked with water that rushes to surprising heights in a dangerously short time. One storm threatened to flood the main floor of La Miniatura after the house was complete, but the home was uninjured and is still one of our national architectural gems.

Wright's structural system evolved in a larger textile block house for Dr. John Storer. He replaced simple wooden molds with more precise and productive aluminum pressure molds. He cast grooves into the sides of these new blocks. They were laid up "dry," without mortar between them, held together by a web of vertical and horizontal steel rods plastered into the grooves.

Wright hoped to use the textile block system as an inexpensive and fireproof medium that could cut costs. If the system were simple enough, the building might not need expensive skilled labor. But there were stubborn problems of leaking and detail. Molded concrete is porous: it soaks up water. Wright never found a way to seal the surfaces so he could prevent seeping from rain or natural springs. Exploring the new system, Wright overran Storer's budget disastrously. Storer lived in the house only three years before it was sold and re-engineered by one of Wright's former draftsmen, Rudolph Schindler.

A house of only 1,500 square feet for Angelenos Samuel and Harriet Freeman was a living proof that "small is beautiful." Wright hungered to build mansions, but he was never more ingenious than when he was coaxing big living areas out of a tiny house. The Freeman walls are a mix of plain blocks and deep-relief blocks carrying one of the square-and-diagonal textures Wright had designed for the Imperial Hotel. But even this petite dwelling overran its budget by 250 percent.

Wright played with the cantilever in all his architecture. He made the jutting roof or balcony into a kind of engineering magic. The Freeman house was the first in which he cantilevered the roof above an open corner of the house. He extended glass windows from both walls so they met at the corner without a wooden mullion (vertical holder). The glass is secured and sealed only by an adhesive. The corner seems to disappear. More peekaboo.

You may have seen parts of the textile block house Wright built for Charles and Mabel Ennis in the movie *Blade Runner*. The movie set for the central character's apartment was built using plaster casts of the Ennis walls.

Even Wright admitted that the California houses had leaks, perhaps worse than most of his roofs. "There are more leaking roofs in California than in the rest of the world put together," he said. "The sun bakes the roof eleven months, two weeks and five days, shrinking it to a shrivel. Then . . . the clouds burst."

Why don't normal houses leak more often? Because they use normal construction methods. Wright dispensed with common, proven details and invented his own. He used untried materials and unusual methods. Many Wright inventions simply didn't work. A client once called him and complained that his roof was leaking. Unmoved, Wright replied, "That's how you know it's a roof."

The textile block problems and the leaking roofs might have been solved by an architect who was on the job to see and correct details. But Wright was most often in Japan or Chicago or Wisconsin. He had never committed himself to California and only visited "his" office there. He had made his son Lloyd a partner in the Los Angeles office, but in name only. Lloyd was intelligent, competent, but not forceful enough to defy his overbearing father. Lloyd was merely a line of communication to clients, a building supervisor, an apologist for mistakes, and a scapegoat. Wright continually blamed him for all the problems Wright had caused. He gave Lloyd the blame for failure but not the authority to avoid it by altering anything. The father was, as usual, scornful of any schedule and lackadaisical about providing crucial drawings. He blamed his son for the delays.

He had not encouraged his children to get a technical or liberal education at a university. Hadn't Wright taught himself everything? Though he was the son and nephew of teachers, he didn't believe in schools, even for very small children. His architect sons were forced to learn the technical demands of the profession "on the job." They didn't share Wright's blithe willingness to lie and sweet-talk his way out of embarrassing mistakes. In the shadow of their father, poorly prepared and less technically knowledgeable than university-trained architects, their confidence was less than sturdy. What scraps of confidence they managed to generate were blown to bits by their father.

In his dealings with his adult children, Frank Lloyd Wright was crueler than William Wright had ever been to him. Wright was quick to find fault, slow to praise, and took all the credit for himself. He accused his children of his own faults and couldn't see their virtues. He used them callously and neglected or even turned on them when they weren't useful.

Wright was a student of Sullivan, who was a student of Jenney. Architectural historians often observe that Wright had no famous students. Neither of the sons who worked closely with him produced extraordinary work on their own. Frank Lloyd Wright seems to have been incapable of passing on his greatness, probably because he was flatly unwilling to share it. His apprentices, students, and children merely carried out his orders and were discouraged from having ideas of their own. Later Wright students built a few homes and public buildings that are generally in his style but none matches the edgy inventiveness, warmth, grace, and brilliant sense of space Wright perfected. It died with him. Perhaps he wanted it that way.

Wright's infatuation with Los Angeles was short and ended with long, acid battles waged by dissatisfied clients.

It was a confusing period for Wright. He had just completed major commissions during a time when many architects were failing. He knew bad times were coming. He was losing the people who were closest to him.

In 1922, Catherine Wright finally abandoned her notion that Frank would return to her and granted him a divorce. In 1919, Aunts Jennie and Nell died at Taliesin. In February of 1923, Anna Wright died. She was a mentally disturbed, aggressively nasty woman who raged at everyone around her, but her life was focused on Frank, only Frank. A few months after Anna's death, to the surprise of virtually every friend and acquaintance, Wright married Miriam Noel.

Why? Her morphine addiction had worsened, and their vicious domestic battles were an angry cycle of suspicion and blame.

If Wright had been driven by the desire for peace and happiness, he wouldn't have married her. But he was driven more powerfully by the desire for familiar feelings that supported his self-image. Wright needed to see himself as a man surrounded by drama and betrayal, dark forces and tragic fate. Miriam fed that melodrama. To give Wright all charity, he was genuinely romantic and believed that Miriam's delusions and addictions could be cured by his love and commitment. Miriam sensed that and used it against him.

The most important man in Wright's life was not his father nor any of his uncles but Louis Sullivan. Wright was surely aware that he was responsible for their separation. Sullivan, always indulgent to his protégé, had soothed Wright's guilt by calling him and chatting warmly in 1918. His *lieber Meister* was once again part of his life. Wright hoped to bring Sullivan out of his alcoholic gloom and back into his rightful place in architecture. Sullivan disappointed him by dying in April of 1924.

Three weeks later Miriam left Wright and Taliesin to live and find new melodrama in Los Angeles.

• 13 •

THE MYSTIC

WRIGHT'S FRESH LOOK at architecture came in the aftermath of World War I, when the world was changing drastically.

In 1914, a single anarchist had assassinated a relatively unimportant Austrian noble. This was the trigger that plunged the entire world into war. World War I was more than battles won and lost. It changed everything. A whole generation was stunned by the horrifying slaughter of the war's great battles. In the stinking trench warfare of Belgium and France, hundreds of thousands of young lives were thrown away. Millions died. Millions more were crippled, injured, ruined by poison gas, mentally broken by shelling. Most of a generation of British, French, Belgian, and German men was cut down. The generals and politicians who drove the war on and on, disregarding casualties, were members of the old order, a senior generation directed by traditional ideas—glory in battle, the beauty of death for one's country, the unquestionable authority of kings and emperors. It wasn't lost on young people that the Great War (as it was called) was waged between three cousins—King George of England, Kaiser Wilhelm of Germany, and Czar Nicholas of Russia, all three grandsons or nephews of Queen Victoria.

Disgust, disbelief, disillusionment—the scarred generation that lived through the First World War could no longer place any faith in the old order of artistic pretensions, traditional styles, or pretty decorations. They were what Gertrude Stein called "the Lost Generation," believing in nothing that wasn't immediate and solid. Modernist writers, painters, and architects threw out old pretty art and pared new art down to the bone. They tried to use harder words, stronger lines. They cast out decoration and concentrated on structure. The machine despised by the British Arts and Crafts Movement became a new god. Modernist architects called for stark machine-made planes and curves, the cold minimum. One ideal of this architecture was what French architect Le Corbusier called "machines for living."

Wright was staggered. He returned from his successes in Japan and California to a new world that denied grace and beauty. He had never been part of the old order. He was always an innovator outside traditional styles. For Wright, the machine could be a tool of beauty and balance, but the "modern" minimalist style had no grace, warmth, beauty, or rhythm. It was cold, antagonistic, daring. For Wright, it had no heart.

The worst post-war shock for Wright was that his own naturally graceful human style was now lumped in with the old order. He was suddenly antique, as dead to the modernist architects as Sullivan. He was a walking ghost of himself.

After Miriam left, Wright was, except for his young draftsmen and their wives, alone. Frank Lloyd Wright couldn't exist alone.

He needed caring for. Without constant care and attention, he'd fall to pieces. It wasn't simply his shirts and meals and household that needed management; Wright needed hour-by-hour attention and adoration.

So it isn't surprising that he spent little time alone after Miriam's departure. What might surprise us is his luck at finding a woman who was the perfect caretaker, guardian, promoter, cheerleader, mistress, wife, and surrogate mother.

On November 22, 1925, Wright attended the Chicago ballet. A slim young woman with dark eyes was shown into the same box. They watched each other as much as the ballet. He invited her for tea afterward and they rose to dance, a waltz. He was fifty-eight, she was twenty-six. She graced, softened, and protected the rest of Wright's long life.

Olga Ivanovna Lazovich Hinzenberg, called Olgivanna, was a great beauty. She had been born in Montenegro, in southeastern Europe. Her father was a Montenegran chief justice and her mother was a general in the Montenegran army, fighting the Turks. The family was intellectual, artistic, professional, politically active. At eighteen she married a Russian architect, Vlademar Hinzenberg. They had a daughter, Svetlana. After only a few years they parted.

The reason for their divorce was a Greek-Armenian cult-leader, Georgei Ivanovitch Gurdjieff (GUHR-jee-ev). Born about 1872, he was a self-proclaimed prophet and mystic who declared that he had traveled all over central Asia learning lost secrets from wise men. He was a startling figure with a shaved head, huge mustache, and piercing, dark eyes. He had been a hypnotist and a fortuneteller, and had promised to teach the meaning of life to those who would follow his directions. Gurdjieff's vague precepts weren't as appealing as his flamboyant style. He set up as a guru and did well. He dismissed most humans as mere sheep. He promised to "awake" his pupils if they followed his strict life of hard work, special meditation, long hours, and dancing. The dancing, inspired by Muslim Sufi, was called "the Movement." The physical stress and psychological mumbo-jumbo was called "The Work." Olgivanna was one of his assistants, and the graceful young woman was among his lead dancers. Olgivanna abandoned her husband for this cult and followed Gurdjieff to France. In 1924, Gurdjieff had an automobile accident near his Institute for the Harmonious Development of Man outside Paris.

Bored with his by then unprofitable organization, he used his injury as an occasion to fire his assistants and disband his followers. When Olgivanna came to Chicago, her divorce from Hinzenberg was almost finalized. She was in the market for another guru.

Both Wright and Gurdjieff were older men, stylish, self-centered, and scornful of the mob. Both were unpredictable, full of pronouncements, quick to anger. They loved fast cars and pretty women. They were loose and foolhardy with money, and both were addicted to drama and flattery.

A few weeks after their meeting, when Wright returned from a trip to his Los Angeles projects, Olgivanna danced at one of Taliesin's musical evenings. Early in 1925, Olgivanna moved into Taliesin with her daughter, Svetlana. She shifted her absolute devotion to her new master.

In the spring of 1925, a knot of faulty telephone wires started another fire at Taliesin. The magnificent living quarters and most of Wright's Asian sculptures, screens, and crafts were destroyed. The real loss was incalculable, but the monetary cost was between $250,000 and $500,000. Wright began immediately on Taliesin

The artist-architect heading for trouble in 1926.

III, the third birth of the same concept, Wright's architectural signature in his Wisconsin home-place.

This fire was only the first of new disasters. Miriam Noel Wright was still legally married to the husband she had left in Wisconsin. She scented the possibility of new drama. It seems likely that she hired private investigators to track Wright and Olgivanna. She discovered that, true to form, Frank had signed himself and Olgivanna in at the Congress Hotel in Chicago as "Mr. & Mrs. Wright." Like most brilliant men he had frequent moments of abysmal stupidity.

Miriam had learned a wonderful trick from Wright's public defense of his relationship with Mamah Cheney: she called a press conference. The scandal-hungry press descended. Miriam described herself as an abandoned wife who had been in California regaining her health. When she was passing through Chicago on her way home to her beloved Taliesen, she happened to pass through the lobby of the Congress Hotel and discovered that the infamously lewd architect was flaunting some "Montenegrin dancer" as Mrs. Wright. And the hussy was pregnant with Wright's child!

The juicy press story got better a month later: Olgivanna gave birth to Iovanna, Wright's daughter, in a Chicago hospital. Miriam tracked them down and forced mother and daughter to flee the hospital carried in a stretcher.

Miriam sued Olgivanna for $100,000, charging her

with alienation of affections, though Wright hadn't met Olgivanna until after Miriam had left him. She also charged that Olgivanna was in the country illegally.

In order to escape the publicity, Wright and Olgivanna left Taliesin. Eventually Wright found a pleasant little cottage on the shores of Lake Minnetonka where he vacationed with Olgivanna, Svetlana, and baby Iovanna. The couple identified themselves as Mr. and Mrs. Frank Richardson, a bow to H. H. Richardson, a friend of Louis Sullivan and an American architect in the era before Wright. But Wright's face was in all the papers, and Miriam had offered a reward for finding him. It wasn't difficult to track a famous man in flashy clothes, driving an unusually expensive car with Wisconsin license plates.

Miriam had already tried to take possession of Taliesin several times. Now, in full swing, she presented herself (with the Chicago reporters) at the gates of Taliesin. She announced that she would move in, fire the staff, and bring in her friends and family. But before Miriam could take up residence at Taliesin, the Bank of Wisconsin, which had been threatening for some time to foreclose on the mortgage they held on the property, announced plans to take possession of the most beautiful home and studio in America. Merchants who had sold Wright building supplies brought a civil suit for payment. The contractors who had supplied labor joined them.

Now Miriam convinced Vlademar Hinzenberg that his own daughter, Svetlana, was in danger. He joined Miriam in her suit against Wright, and Miriam also instituted new Mann Act charges against Wright.

A few weeks later, federal and state officers, accompanied by Miriam's lawyer, burst into the vacation home and arrested them for Mann Act violations, adultery, and other charges. They went to jail, the children went into custody, and Miriam went into raptures of delight.

This situation would have been the pit of despair for many people. Wright, however, had that creative and egotistic disengagement that armored him against normal disaster. It wasn't crisis he feared; it was boredom. In court the next day he was reported as looking jaunty and humorous, swinging his cane with a bouncy arrogance. Olgivanna looked awful. He and

Olgivanna were released on bail and they returned to Chicago.

To hold off the loss of Taliesin, Wright proposed to sell off his stock of Japanese prints. It was a rich trove of art, probably the best Japanese collection in the country and increasing in value, since the emperor had restricted the sale of art treasures outside Japan. The assessed value was more than $100,000, but the New York auction netted only $36,975. The shockingly low prices paid for the art should have warned Wright of a serious turn in the national economy, but financial matters big or small were beneath his notice.

Neither Wright nor the bank received any of the money. Wright had neglected to mention to the bank that, in his usual double-dipping way, he had already borrowed about $35,000 on the prints from the gallery auctioning them. The gallery's bill was $37,000.

The bank had taken possession of Taliesin. They were using it to store records, but local folks broke in repeatedly and "took souvenirs." The bank announced the property would be sold at auction. The *Chicago Tribune* gleefully published a fake advertisement: "For Sale: one romantic, rambling, famous picturesque home on a hill with 190 acres of farm and park, known as a 'love nest,' murder scene, fire scene, raid scene and showplace."

Back to the wall, Wright hired the best civil lawyer in Wisconsin: Philip F. La Follette, a familiar name in the state. His father had been governor and was, at the time, a United States Senator. (Philip, himself, would also be governor.) He shared Wright's intelligence but not much else: unlike Wright he was cautious, patient, careful, and quiet. He became Wright's legal conscience and his unseen leash for years. Philip La Follette saved Frank Lloyd Wright from legal ruin, laying out for Wright all the unappetizing courses he had to take. It was a thankless job. Wright abused him as if the lawyer were responsible for the encroaching legal realities. La Follette shrugged Wright's fussiness off and managed over several years to defuse Miriam's overblown claims. In the end she made a stinging but final settlement of divorce. La Follette used calm, horsetrader negotiations with the Bank of Wisconsin and Wright's Wisconsin creditors. He persuaded the bank to give Wright a year's grace. The bank bought Taliesin at auction for $25,000 (it was the only bidder) and was willing to sell it back to Wright for $60,000. La Follette backed them down to $40,000; $15,000 in cash and (La Follette must have hypnotized them to extend credit to Wright again) a $25,000 mortgage. The building material suppliers settled for a reduced sum and the contractors extended their credit. Wright was reinstalled in Taliesin.

Wright, of course, didn't pay La Follette's bill.

Wright had a brilliant notion at the brink of disaster: sell himself! Wright proposed a legal sale: make Frank Lloyd Wright a corporation and sell shares in his future profits to wealthy investors. If he could find ten investors to put up $7,500 each, he could be saved from his own folly.

His old friends and clients, for reasons we might have difficulty understanding, bought him. It was 1928, he was now a capitalized corporation, Wright Inc., and, once again, saved in the nick of time. Temporarily.

• 14 •

THE GREAT DEPRESSION

AFTER THE LAWSUITS and losses, Frank Lloyd Wright turned his unsinkable enthusiasm toward several promising large scale projects.

The Arizona Biltmore was to be built in the vast Mojave Desert of the Southwest, new territory for Wright. It was meant as a posh spa for the wealthy. Two brothers, Albert and Charles McArthur, were the organizers. Charles was an architect. Officially, he asked Wright only to be a consultant in the use of textile block construction for the desert Biltmore. Wright consented to "license" the use of his textile block method. This was a bit of flimflammery because Wright had no patent on the method (patent holders for similar systems would later sue the McArthurs for patent infringement). Nor was Wright an expert in the actual construction: he had always delegated the site supervision to Lloyd Wright. But Wright needed the money, wanted to see a very large structure built with the system, and accepted. He approved new patterns for blocks and the production of the necessary 250,000 concrete blocks began.

It's possible that McArthur asked Wright for the design of the hotel, too. Historians and architectural critics disagree on the hand behind the Arizona Biltmore. Wright needed quick cash and had become wary of patent fights with his not entirely original textile block system. For a hefty consultant's fee he almost undoubtedly designed the Biltmore but insisted in a legal document that Charles McArthur had been the architect. The spaces, textures, layout, and details are so like the Imperial Hotel's that there is no doubt Wright at least collaborated. The individual cottages that are part of the complex are close siblings to La Miniatura. It is equally obvious, however, that McArthur revised Wright's design in many ways. He almost certainly lifted the ceilings in many places. (Wright was famous for ceiling heights that actually bump the heads of even modestly tall basketball players.)

Several other new commissions had also arisen as possibilities. The National Life Insurance Company asked him to design a skyscraper. Though he loudly despised the modern city and the skyscraper as inhuman, he tried his hand at the vertical theme. Promoter Gordon Strong asked Wright to design a structure for Sugarloaf Mountain, Maryland, one of the highest peaks in the Appalachians. It was to be a kind of automobile "lookout." Automobile tourists were a new phenomenon of American life, so Wright called it an "automobile objective" and designed a tall, inward-ramping double spiral. The spiral was creeping into Wright's design vocabulary.

Neither the National Life skyscraper nor "The Automobile Objective" would be built, but parts of their designs reappeared later. Frank Lloyd Wright never threw out ideas; he merely postponed them.

St. Mark's-in-the-Bouwerie was to be a set of three residential skyscrapers surrounding historic St. Mark's church in lower Manhattan. Wright also prepared sketches for a million-member, all-steel cathedral, about as practical as a colony on Mars. These projects remained unbuilt as well, but their designs were tucked away for later use.

Why were promoters and high-flyers pursuing Wright? As the saying goes, "No publicity is bad publicity." Whether or not Wright was considered a cad, sex-maniac, deadbeat, or part of the old order, he was the most famous architect in the world. Why not cash in on his reputation?

Another project in Arizona was San Marcos-in-the-Desert, a high-ticket resort. Its promoter, veterinarian Dr. Albert Chandler, was a good match for Wright. He bubbled with zest and optimism. He had acquired a spectacular site in the desert near Phoenix and chose Wright as the only American architect who could do it justice. He wanted something like a pleasure city to lure the Eastern wealthy to bake and play in the unfailing sun of the Mojave. The commission Wright was offered would run to $40,000, not as much as the Imperial Hotel commission but a welcome sum after the trials and troubles he had endured.

Dr. Chandler's San Marcos-in-the-Desert concept was up in the air waiting for backers who would surely come. He was eager for Wright's plans and renderings to attract them, so he suggested that Wright come to Arizona and work on the site.

Wright's friends had sunk large sums of money into Frank Lloyd Wright as a corporation and given him back his dear Taliesin in 1928. But to lawyer La Follette's horror, and without consulting the investors in the fledgling corporation, Wright left Taliesin on January 28, 1929, during a howling Wisconsin blizzard. He headed for Arizona with all his "boys" and equipment.

The desert changed the way he saw and worked. Its broad scale stunned him. The raw edginess of the crags, mountains, rifts, and ridges shifted his perspective. The rich, unexpected earth colors excited him. But most impressive, most powerful was the desert light: it thrummed and glared, it was integral with the harsh but embracing heat, it dominated and demanded. Wright gave a large part of himself to the desert.

In his usual way, Wright would not pick up a pencil until he established a princely base of operations. Ignoring La Follette's pleas for economy, he ordered truckloads of building material, furniture, food, and rugs, and rented a grand piano. He and the boys built a camp unlike any other. The walls were stained, rough-sawn wood and local rubble stone in concrete. The roofs were stretched tan canvas that caught the light and passed it on as a diffuse, pervading, magical glow to the drafting tables below. Stone firepits were the centers of their evening gatherings. Wright called the camp Ocatillo, after the hardy desert plant.

From January to June they worked on the San Marco project, creating plans and renderings to make the project ready to receive bids from contractors.

In late June, the market and the economy were uncertain. Investors hadn't appeared, but Chandler was certain it was just a matter of a month or so. Wright sent the boys back to Taliesin and moved on to New York to discuss St. Mark's-in-the-Bouwerie. He designed three towers, two of fifteen stories, one of twenty stories. Each was constructed around a central pinwheel core. He saw the core as the trunk of a tree. Like a tree, the structure was anchored deep in the earth by a "taproot" foundation. The core contained elevators to reach the floors, and provided the strength and stability. Each floor was cantilevered from the trunk, so the glass and metal cladding on the exterior was a light, pierced shell rather than a heavy wall. It was beautiful and it was brilliant instinctive engineering.

But the year was drawing to an end, and bad times were on their way.

There are cycles overlaying American history: religious frenzies springing up every few decades, people moving west to settle the American frontier in ragged pulses. The United States economy had risen and fallen many times in an irregular but repeating cycle, but no one financial event had ever threatened every American.

Economics deals with numbers but isn't mathematically neat. Too much hinges on what people do and how they feel. What Americans *think* is as powerful as the numbers. So when we look back at the Great Depression, the biggest stumble in American economic history, the causes and remedies are all "maybes."

There was a building boom in the mid-1920s that created an oversupply of homes and a slowdown of construction jobs at the end of the decade. World War I demanded food for soldiers, farmers borrowed money for more land and equipment, then food prices dropped steeply. Small, local banks weren't as stable or well backed as big city banks. Boom-time optimism encouraged everyone to buy and sell shares on the stock market. It all made sense. But in the fall of 1929 people were buying less. When people stopped buying, merchants stopped ordering new stock. Factories cut back on production and laid off employees. More people were now unemployed, so they bought even less. A snowball was starting down a steep hill, picking up speed and weight.

Sometime in late 1929, some stock market investors began to see that the economy was slowing. They sold their stock before the prices fell. A rush of other investors followed them. Stock prices plunged. Small investors were forced to sell all their stocks. The market began to slide. Large investors sold huge blocks of stock. Prices fell even more.

On October 24, 1929, the New York Stock Exchange was nearly wiped out. Prices hit bottom. Stock brokers call this awful day Black Thursday.

The stock market crash wasn't the only reason for the economic crash. It was a symptom, one result of the snowball effect of the economy rumbling down faster and faster.

Panic. People stopped buying new things, building new houses, investing money in businesses. Factories fired millions of workers. Mortgage holders couldn't pay their monthly amounts; banks foreclosed on mortgages; farms, houses, businesses were taken away.

Panic pushed some people to withdraw all their money from their banks. Banks invest the money they take in; they don't have it all in their vaults. In the next few years there were thousands of "runs" on banks, caused by sheer fright. When enough depositors lined up and demanded all their money, the banks—even well-funded and well-run banks—failed.

Within months a larger part of the American population was out of work than ever before—or since. One of every five Americans had no job. Hundreds of thousands had lost their homes. Farmers were forced off their land. The citizens of the United States began to doubt their government's ability to keep the country together.

The Federal Reserve System had been set up to adjust the economy through interest rates and the sale of government bonds so this kind of panic wouldn't happen. But the powerful head of the Federal Reserve had just died, and no one had taken charge quickly.

The president of the United States, Herbert Hoover, was a smart, honest, competent administrator. He was an engineer who had accomplished great things, but he was powerless against the rolling snowball. Homeless people threw up shantytowns of scrap material as temporary houses; they called them "Hoovervilles."

Hoover lost the next election to Franklin Delano Roosevelt, who promised to bring the United States back to prosperity. He knew the prime evil was panic. He said, "We have nothing to fear but fear, itself."

The country had plunged into despair and confusion. There was no new building. Buildings already planned were scrapped. Architecture was dead.

Frank Lloyd Wright, like every other architect in America, had almost no commissions. Plans for St. Mark's-in-the-Bouwerie were dropped. Hopes for San Marcos-in-the-Desert were only a beautiful set of drawings. Though it was one of Wright's most charming creations, there were no financial backers, and the commission was on the shelf. For all his work on San Marcos and Ocatillo, Wright (and, technically, the shareholders in Frank Lloyd Wright, Incorporated) were out-of-pocket for $19,000. Even Ocatillo disappeared, board by board. The lumber and the canvas were quietly, usefully salvaged by local Indians for their home repairs, and by spring hardly a trace was left. The only thing that remained of the desert base was impressive photographs being published in European architectural magazines. The lines and shapes and light patterns of an unmistakably original desert architecture were keenly appreciated in Europe.

The Wright corporation was moot, no longer valid. It had existed as a friendly willingness on the part of responsible friends to help Wright and be part of his whirling generation of creative ideas. But as a reality it was impossible: Frank Lloyd Wright was a singularity, a phenomenon that couldn't be extended, reduced, duplicated, or altered. Though he was willing to accept money and adulation, he was incapable of sharing his private pinnacle. Wright had the curious notion that his stockholders owed *him*. Why weren't they supporting him as they should be? Why were his accounts empty when he had stockholders? La Follette explained that his view of corporate financial flow was backward and once again asked Wright to pay him for his crucial work. Wright was offended and naturally refused to pay the man who saved him.

Another casualty of the Depression was D. D. Martin, Wright's genial friend and constant lender. Martin—of course he was one of the shareholders in Frank Lloyd Wright, Incorporated—had inextinguishable patience for his madcap, imprudent friend. No one would ever be as forgiving and faithfully supportive as Martin. The Depression wiped out his entire fortune. Wright had designed him a gravesite setting they jokingly called the Martin Blue Sky Mausoleum. There was no money left to build it. When Martin died in 1935, he was buried in an unmarked grave.

Wright had an advantage in these difficult times: he had always been in financial crisis. Nothing new here. Furthermore, he didn't care a hoot about money, only what it could do for him. If he got it, he spent it. He spent it even when he *didn't* get it.

He was still the most famous architect in the world. Famous for the buildings he'd completed, surely, but also for Wright designs that had never been built. He wasn't famous for the money he'd made. Some other architects were wealthy, some had designed more buildings than Wright. The extraordinary and unmistakable thing about Frank Lloyd Wright was that he saw, thought, and designed at a level no other architect could even consider. Wright basically ignored the real world and lived in a fantasy of his own creation, but his work was irresistibly appealing. As a promoter of his work, Wright himself was irresistible. A friend said, in wonder, "He was two hundred percent alive." His friend Alexander Woolcott, the wit and pundit of the Algonquin Roundtable, wrote a profile of Wright for *The New Yorker*, saying, "If the editor of this journal were so to ration me that I were suffered to apply the word 'genius' to only one living American, I would have to save it for Frank Lloyd Wright."

Olgivanna had a heavier influence on Wright's public image and his decisions than his former wives and mistresses. Becoming Gurdjieff's assistant had been an education in dealing with prophets and mystics. She played Wright like a violin. Flattering, reassuring, reminding, she softened his flaming temper and encouraged him to use his theatrical posturing to profitable effect as an architectural authority and lecturer. Throughout the Depression, Wright lectured at hundreds of schools, conferences, meetings, and workshops for minor but welcome fees. To everyone's delight, he usually insulted the local architecture. About Pittsburgh, Pennsylvania, he said, "It would probably be cheaper to abandon it than rebuild it." Asked what to do with Boston, he said, "Bury it!"

She also prodded him to finish a project he had toyed with since 1926: an autobiography. She knew it could be a therapeutic task, putting many demons and disappointments to rest by rephrasing and, yes, even rewriting them.

Olgivanna had developed other skills at the Institute for the Harmonious Development of Man. She was an expert organizer of disciples. She and Frank conceived a brilliant scheme: the Taliesin Fellowship. They sent a letter to schools and universities in 1932, full of high-sounding words and solemn damnations of most architectural education, offering the opportunity to work and live at Taliesin with like-minded apprentices. The students would live a communal life of creativity and hard work, sharing the chores of the farm and home, building and drafting under the master. It wasn't an accredited school. Apprentices would receive no degree or credits toward a degree in any other school. There was no set curriculum of study. The beauty of the plan, for the Wrights, was that young people paid *them* to work. For the privilege of being near the great Frank Lloyd Wright, they would pay only $650 a year and four hours of labor each day. The following year the tuition rose to $1,100. The first group of thirty-three apprentices responded.

The apprentices were largely what we would call dropouts today—young people dissatisfied with the rigor of traditional universities. They were students who rankled at required technical classes in strength of materials, integral calculus, and other engineering tools. Some were disappointed by university study of classic Roman and Greek styles.

It wasn't a traditional education. Many of the aspiring architects were learning more about tending the animals and weeding the fields than about design. They constructed new buildings and maintained existing buildings, cooked in the kitchen, served at the table, and performed in frequent "entertainments" as dancers and musicians. Only a few were allowed to draft the master's designs. It was a catch-as-catch-can learning arrangement, and a successful stay at Taliesin was no guarantee of a welcoming reception in the profession. Indeed, association with the Fellowship was often a drawback: architects and engineers admired Wright's achievements but not his methods or his attitudes.

The Fellowship had a distinct "inside" group. Those who adopted Gurdjieff's work and movement—quasi-mystical spirituality—were given special attention by Olgivanna and special access to the master. Any number of infractions could send an apprentice packing. Critical discussion of the master's precepts and pronouncements was not welcome. Like Taliesin itself, the Fellowship was an atmosphere contrived by Wright; both had roots in the medieval and renaissance Italian villas he loved, complete with their master-and-subject society.

The meals were simple country fare because there was almost no cash to buy provisions. A case of lettuce in midwinter was a jubilant treat for all. Soup with cabbage and potatoes was often on the menu, but Olgivanna never allowed the quality of the dining to be compromised by the humbleness of the dinner. There were always greenhouse flowers, music, beautifully set and decorated tables, and a royal atmosphere centered on the master.

It wasn't an equal band of brothers and sisters and it wasn't exactly an education. But it was an unforgettable experience. Wright said to a friend that life at Taliesin was "a democracy. When I'm hungry, everyone eats."

The Fellowship gave Wright access to a workforce he couldn't otherwise find in the hills of Wisconsin. It gave him a crew of "experimental" builders to try new techniques and materials on the Taliesin structures, and an inexhaustible supply of servants. It gave him another invaluable mainstay: family. He had adopted Svetlana, and Iovanna was growing, but even his family of six children with Catherine hadn't been a true comfort; they weren't focused directly on him. Now, however, he had his small army of apprentices, thirty-three young men and women, collectively referred to as the "boys," who ate with him, worked with him, and hung on his every word. It wasn't a family so much as a kingdom.

In 1932 the Museum of Modern Art in New York mounted an exhibit organized by Henry-Russell

Hitchcock and architect Philip Johnson. It was at this exhibit that the label "International Style" was coined, embracing the minimalist designs of Walter Gropius, Mies van der Rohe, and Charles-Édouard Jeanneret, known as Le Corbusier. Wright contributed a design for "a house on the mesa," exploring his new fascination with the desert, but he was not kind to his colleagues, considering them little more than thieves of his basic work. They saw it differently, and rendered him great respect.

An Autobiography was published in a small printing of 2,500 in 1932 and was a surprise best seller. The initial printing was almost immediately sold out. The second printing of 10,000 sold out as well. It was deceptive, self-serving, bombastic, and the concepts were so hazy as to be undefinable, but the public loved it.

He was out of work, eating potato-and-cabbage soup, and scrounging for every nickel. At the same time he was spending like a drunken sailor. He trudged from one city to another, lecturing in drafty auditoriums but dressed in custom-tailored tweeds. Penniless, nearing sixty-five, proud as a peacock, and mocking defeat, Frank Lloyd Wright was still a powerful force.

• 15 •

SHAKING IT OUT OF HIS SLEEVE

WHAT SHAPES THE direction of a design to bring forth a barn or a church or a prison? The seed is an architectural *program*: the set of a structure's requirements, what it must accomplish, services it must provide, the restrictions of the site, the needs of the clients, the budget, the local building codes, the deadline. The best designers discover that restrictions don't discourage creativity; they drive it.

Homes often have the most complex programs. Think of all the activities that go on in a home. Think of how different one family is from another—one family is full of sports fans, another full of musicians. What can a house do to support the people who live in it? How can a house encourage a comfortable, fulfilling life?

Frank Lloyd Wright is especially celebrated for his residence designs. He should be, because he changed the over-formal, dark, and traditionally fixed formula of American houses to a brighter and looser understanding of "home." He celebrated the hearth and the dining room as "altars" to the spirit of family. In this way he was a breakthrough innovator. His approach to the subject was, however, more abstract than particular; he thought more about his own style than the individual people who lived with it. Sometimes his homes fit the owners like a custom-tailored suit. Other homes were beautiful, but didn't fit their owners' lives, budgets, or special needs. Wright cared less about the program than about an achievement of style.

One way he excused himself (expertly) was by asserting that the business of the architect was to re-educate the client. In some ways he was right. Residential clients had to be led away from their social reliance on formally boxed-in dining rooms and parlors, Roman columns, and meaningless decorations. An architect could bring a fresh perspective to the program of a residence. But the needs of a family—their work, patterns of life, ways of entertaining, ages, and budget—were essential in a home's program. Wright too often ignored their personal realities.

Lecturing in Dallas, Texas, Wright met Stanley Marcus, who sold men's clothing. (He would later be famous as the co-owner of Neiman-Marcus.) Wright's work excited him and he happened to mention that he and his wife planned to build a home in the Texas hill country for something around $45,000.

Ridiculous, Wright sniffed. He would design a home for Marcus that would cost no more than $10,000. Marcus was delighted. A Frank Lloyd Wright home. And a bargain!

Wright made a visit to the Marcus land in the middle of December, on a freakishly warm day. "Why Stanley, you have better weather here in Dallas than they do in Arizona!"

No, Marcus explained, mild temperatures in this part of Texas were rare in December.

A few months later Wright sent the designs for a fine home. But it had no bedrooms. Marcus pointed out this odd oversight.

Wright replied that in such a wonderful climate, they should sleep outside!

Marcus explained, once again, that the winters were really quite harsh.

Wright grudgingly added bedrooms but they had no closets. Marcus wrote that he wanted closets.

Ridiculous, Wright replied, Marcus should get rid of all the clothes he would hang in a closet.

Marcus replied patiently that he sold men's clothing and was obliged to dress well as a matter of business.

Wright added closets.

Back and forth, bit by bit, the design was approved and went out for bids. The cheapest bid for building the Marcus house was $150,000.

Marcus was shocked. He called Wright, reminding him that he had proposed a $10,000 house. Wright replied that contractors overbid because they couldn't read the plans correctly.

"Whose fault is that?" Marcus shot back, "Yours or theirs?"

Stung, Wright said that he, himself, would build the house for a fixed amount.

Fine, Marcus allowed, but would he guarantee the price and pay anything over it?

Wright had backed himself into a corner. He flew into a righteous rage and demanded all the drawings back. The commission was dropped.

A few years later Marcus sent Wright a photograph of a house he'd had built by a local architect for a reasonable price. Wright sent a brief, acid note: "Dear Stanley: I didn't think you would be satisfied with so little."

Edgar J. Kaufmann, Jr., was a member of the Wright Fellowship. He'd studied painting and architecture in America and Europe but, like many of the other apprentices, was not quite certain where he fit in the arts. After a year he realized that the cult-like Fellowship experience didn't suit him, but he invited his parents to meet the great Frank Lloyd Wright.

Wright had a bloodhound's nose for money. Edgar J. Kaufmann, Sr., owned a large and prosperous department store in Pittsburgh, Pennsylvania. In his role as princely host of Taliesin, Wright mesmerized Kaufmann. Soon, he was trying to get Wright commissions in Pittsburgh. He also had the great man design his own office at the department store. It was an elaborate design and took two years to complete. The result was so splendid that when the building was demolished, the office was taken apart and re-created as an exhibit at the Victoria and Albert Museum in London, England.

In the winter of 1935, Kaufmann had a whimsical notion: he suggested that Wright build him a summer place on a bit of woodland property in southern Pennsylvania. It was dear to the family because of a picturesque waterfall along a robust little stream called Bear Run. There the creek tumbled over massive boulders on which the family liked to sunbathe, cooling themselves in the pools below the falls. Wright visited the site, poked about, and agreed to build a house with a budget of $20,000 to $30,000. Not surprisingly, the old magician moved on to other projects without much more than a glance at the topographic site map Kaufmann had sent.

The following September, Kaufmann, impatient for some design results, called from Milwaukee. He was on a business trip to the Midwest and he could come by Taliesin to look at the summer home design.

To the surprise of everyone in the drafting room,

Wright said, "Come along, E. J.! We're ready for you!"

The next morning, Kaufmann called to say he was on his way. Not a line had been drawn for the design. Kaufmann was two hours and twenty minutes away.

A table was cleared, the site map taped down. Wright stepped up to the board and began to work in a pleasant state of mind. He worked on tracing paper, as architects do, so the lines of drawings beneath can guide the layer above them. He worked quickly, talking to himself, using the traditional tools of the architect—T-square, triangle, pencils, and erasers. His apprentices sharpened new pencils as he dulled them with his busy lines and cast them aside. He erased, brushed the dust away, redrew. A plan, a shape, a conception gradually appeared on the paper like a ghost emerging from a cloud. It was something whole and strong and exciting. It came together as if it were a favorite scene drawn from memory, and yet it was like nothing Frank Lloyd Wright had ever designed in form or structure or engineering principle.

When Kaufmann arrived, Wright had drawn the plans for two floors, two elevations, a section, and a perspective drawing of a home he named, at the bottom of the drawings, "Fallingwater." The design never changed. Kaufmann was thrilled. Everyone in the drafting room was thrilled.

Almost as impressive as the magically produced design was Wright's explanation of its principles and virtues. He rattled on like a revival tent preacher, as if he had practiced this sermon to Kaufmann for weeks. Architect and client took a break, leaving for the upper terrace of Taliesin for a bite of lunch. While they were dining, two apprentices hurried to finish two missing

Fallingwater, Bear Run, Pennsylvania.

elevations in Wright's style and slip them under the earlier sheets. When Wright returned, he resumed his talk and flourished the drawings as if they'd always been there.

This sudden, virtuoso design event, repeated occasionally with other projects, was what Wright called "shaking a design out of my sleeve." If the apprentices weren't witnesses to this strange event, it would sound like one of the Frank Lloyd Wright fictions he spun.

Many creative geniuses—composers, scientists, painters, writers—have noted a similar outpouring of certainty, an ease of invention after ignoring a project for weeks or months. They looked at the outlines of a project, understood the problems to be solved, noted all its parts . . . and then forgot it. Their conscious minds applied themselves to present things. Their subconscious minds were somehow at work on the solution. And so it must have been with Wright. It was the rarest kind of creation, the birth of an American icon—a shape or a look that becomes a part of our shared artistic culture. In his career Wright would create half a dozen icons, but Fallingwater may be the most distinctive and compelling.

Its beauty is bold. Against the dim and infinitely textured eastern woodland, its strong planes strike out over the water, declaring the dominance of geometry over forest chaos. The rounded boulders are rooted deep in the ravine of Bear Run, but the light-colored walls of the house and porches seem to float without support. Fallingwater doesn't crouch over the waterfall but becomes a part of it, some mathematical expression of solidity leaping exuberantly out of tired, water-worn granite.

Its engineering is daring. Wright was always edging into new technology, and in Fallingwater he leaped into reinforced concrete.

Reinforced concrete was the invention of a French gardener. He made large flowerpots strengthened with steel wire inside the cast concrete. The two materials have interlocking strengths: concrete is wonderfully strong in compression (pushing), while steel is strong in tension (pulling). Wright was just beginning to explore the possibilities. As a first proof of principles, Fallingwater is a triumph.

This was one of the first homes to utilize the versatile material that became a mainstay of Wright's work. The impressive cantilevers, supported in the dimness below the planes, stretch out and out without apparent support. But the structure is built in, because Wright used the *parapets*—the walls at the edges of the porches—as vertical beams. These stout beams resist the downward bending forces.

Deep in the Great Depression, Frank Lloyd Wright catapulted himself once again into the predominant position as leader of American architecture. Fallingwater was famous before it was even finished in 1935: drawings of it were run in the architectural magazines to international delight.

Kaufmann, himself, had a few reservations. He had requested that the home have a *view* of the waterfall. As designed, the house was *over* the waterfall. Wright brushed this aside, saying that he didn't want the family to merely *look* at the waterfall but to *live* with it.

Head Fellowship apprentice Wes Peters and Chicago engineer Mendel Glickman supervised the engineering details, but Kaufmann was doubtful. He quietly showed the plans to a firm of Pittsburgh engineers. They questioned the boulders on which Wright built the house. Were they stable or would they turn over? They also doubted that the cantilevers would hold up and called for more steel. When Kaufmann showed the engineers' report to Wright, he was furious. He demanded all the drawings back, he was finished with Kaufmann, the man didn't *deserve* a Wright home! Kaufmann apologized and the construction continued. (But Kaufmann quietly added more steel to the builder's structural plans.)

No other American home is as sheltering and strikingly beautiful as Fallingwater. It is genius. Nothing else is like it, no other home has its bold but human style. It creates it own order in the forest and arranges the landscape around it: we can't imagine moving it anywhere else; we can't imagine the place, those boulders and that cascade of water, without it. Fallingwater is one of our national treasures.

We can quibble with Wright's lack of common sense, financial responsibility, political awareness, or even good manners, but we can't argue about the treasures he shook out of his sleeve.

• 16 •

DE/ERT LORD

WRIGHT SEEMED UNSTOPPABLE, immortal, keeping up a furious jig of work, travel, writing, entertainments, and lectures. He tired out his apprentices and exhausted his clients, but in the winter of 1936 he was approaching seventy and his health had never been reliable.

He went down hard that winter with pneumonia. Antibiotics hadn't been developed. A severe bacterial infection of the lungs was more responsive to good nursing than good doctoring. His life was genuinely threatened for months.

The flaw in the Taliesin Fellowship was thrown into sharp focus: no one but Taliesin's own *lieber Meister* could make decisions, alter designs to fit new situations, or respond with solutions to new problems. Every project ground to a standstill.

When Wright returned to the drafting room in mid-January of 1937, his hours were still limited and his lungs were still delicate. The Wisconsin winters were dangerous for an old man. He remembered the clean, dry heat of Arizona and the shimmering light on the desert from his vanished camp at Ocatillo. He was convinced that winters in Arizona would save his lungs and his life. He was also excited by the intense light of the desert. Undeterred by the Depression or by his lack of capital, he set out with Olgivanna and "the boys" to create a second Taliesin in the West.

He bought an expanse of the Sonoran Desert from the government at $3.50 an acre—800 acres of barren, remote waste—and began to order building materials again.

As a building site, his acreage was as close to a blank slate as possible. A duller mind would not have found much inspiration there. The planes of the desert were subtle. The rusty, dusty, bleached colors clustered in a narrow range. It was all horizon: horizontal planes grooved by arroyos, low shrub, scoured boulders, and made to seem even flatter by occasional spurs of exposed rock. For verticals he had only distant mountain slopes approximating his drafting tool, the 30°-60°-90° triangle, and the incongruous saguaro cactus with its spiked cartoon arms.

In his usual mysterious and hypnotic way, he convinced local businesspeople that they should be honored to extend him credit. Lots of credit.

The first necessity was water. There was no water in sight and no history of water anywhere nearby, so he summoned a driller to sink a well-pipe into the desert floor. The rig was erected as the apprentices began to work on the drafting room and living quarters. The rig kept drilling, day after day, cutting into the rock basin slowly and hopefully, down and down, trailing a hundred feet of pipe, two hundred. Water was finally found and brought up to create Frank Lloyd Wright's own oasis. The well cost $10,000.

It was not exactly "adapting to the site" as Wright preached. In real practice, he wrestled a site into his power. Wright's "organic" architecture sometimes required enormous inorganic fuel and machinery to master the land.

But many of his adaptations were ingenious.

He took a cue from the thick walls of the south-west's indigenous architectural form, the adobe house. These massive walls were built of cheap, heavy, sun-baked adobe brick mixed from mud and straw. They were laid up with rubble and mud plaster as in-sloping walls with a thick cross-section that retained the cool of the desert nights through the day. By night-fall they had absorbed the sun's warmth and passed it on through the night.

Wright's walls were also massive, made largely of angular, flat-sided stones dragged from the acreage on a sheet-steel "stone boat" by one of several Caterpil-lar tractors. The big stones were laid up in wooden wall-forms and bound together by "desert concrete"—cement mixed with the site's sand. The colors and char-acter of the walls came from the desert floor itself.

The new Taliesin was a long, low prism. Angular vertical walls were spaced out over nine hundred feet, backed by a low, connecting horizontal wall. Redwood beams covered by natural canvas panels spanned these verticals. The angles mirrored the angles of the moun-tain ridges: low against a rear buttress wall, rising to a shallow peak, falling more abruptly in a shed roof to the open side. The natural canvas filtered, softened, but passed on the light as it had at Ocatillo.

As it rose they began to call it "Taliesin West." It began as a camp and continued in serial building spurts each winter.

As the Wisconsin cold closed down on Taliesin East, the *lieber Meister* would set the day of their departure. They left like some nomadic carnival, usually in the middle of a blizzard, moving south and west in a caravan of trucks and cars with "the boys," their wives, the cook, servants. Wright and Olgivanna were out ahead, scouting locations for lunches and camps. They circled up the vehicles like a wagon train and built a fire (always the sacred fire) in the center to cook provisions, or they accepted the hospitality of architects and architecture professors along the route.

The provisions were bought at a local Spring Green store, revealing one of Wright's rare sensible financial habits. He'd established an exclusive relationship with the owner. Taliesin shopped at no other grocers in Wisconsin, and she extended unlimited credit. One by one the back bills were paid, even as new supplies were purchased. The owner declared, "I never lost a cent on Frank Wright and don't intend to."

The drafting room at Taliesin West was a delight. The complex but orderly redwood trusses that spanned the spaces created a forest canopy of connected limbs. Translucent canvas and high clerestory windows made the space glow with a gentle, workable light. At the end of the drafting room was, naturally, a grand fireplace against the surprisingly cool desert nights. Reflecting pools and fountains splashed outside. Cooking, serenading, games, and discussion were carried on as much outside on the broad terraces as inside. The terraces were surrounded by a margin of broken rock. Visitors didn't often recognize its function: to discourage desert rattlesnakes from crossing onto the terraces and slithering about the living spaces. The rocks didn't discourage the scorpions, however, and there were plenty of these.

Apprentices and draftsmen had rooms off the workroom, or they built tents and outbuildings for themselves. The main living space was given over to communal dinners, the master's quarters, and a good-time space in which visitors were entertained by the nightly recitals—music, readings, plays, and dancing.

And yet again, Frank Lloyd Wright created another American icon—this one in the middle of the barren desert. Taliesin West was a healthy cure for Wright, but it became a sought-after invitation, a destination for the famous, a lure for prospective clients, a magical place. No other architect or artist created such a stylish, substantial setting for his theatrical presence. The idea alone was brilliant. But the quality of the space and the genius of the design was incomparably Wright.

• 17 •

DANGEROUS DREAM

THE CATASTROPHES OF the First World War and the Great Depression had upset an ugly bucket of political wrangling in Europe. Hundreds of parties and movements squabbled for the hearts of discontented, doubtful people. There were ideas of every flavor, but they generally sorted themselves into two opposite political directions: socialism, which planned to place power in the hands of more people and rely on mankind's natural idealism; and fascism, which invested total power in the hands of a few strong people to make tough decisions in a cruel world.

In financially ruined Germany, the fascist National Socialist (Nazi) party and its spellbinding leader, Adolf Hitler, blamed Germany's troubles on Jews and Communists.

Russian communism began as socialist idealism. But under the guise of a liberal ideal, communism had been made into a new form of fascism in the enormous Soviet Union by a ruthless leader, Joseph Stalin.

This fascist/socialist struggle was felt in the United States, but in a different way. The Great Depression raised suspicions in working-class Americans. They blamed the broken economy on big business and leaned toward socialist ideas like state-owned utilities and banks, a system of "social security" for elders (still in place), and strong unions on socialist models. At the other end of the financial spectrum, the great American corporations advocated stronger government controls. The distant ends were uneasily tied together by the reassuring voice of President Franklin Delano Roosevelt and his "New Deal," which used both socialist welfare features and strong federal controls.

Against the ideological background of fascism and socialism, Wright conceived an idea of social reform with the best—and worst—of both: Broadacre City.

Reform by social planning was an active theme of the 1930s. The Soviet communes were "scientifically" laid out with maximum production in mind. Soviet social design extended to ideal state-run nurseries and maximum-efficiency workers' uniforms. The French architect Le Corbusier's Ville Radieuse was a cluster of high-rise apartment houses in a park setting, his approach to maximizing production by grouping many workers near factories.

Wright despised Le Corbusier and his "machine for living" modernism. Wright's idea of social good was what worked for him. Every citizen should reject the soiled, unhealthy, spiritually bankrupt city and share Wright's green idyll. Every man should have his own Taliesin.

True to his Arts and Crafts roots, he proposed a return to country living and the ancient mystical values of the soil. In the same way, early British Arts and Crafts reformers had built utopian "workers' villages" to lead the lower classes out of the city slums into the fresh air.

Wright and his apprentices, with a grant from Edgar J. Kaufmann, constructed a model of Wright's utopia twelve feet square. It was a charming miniature world exhibited at the Industrial Arts Exhibition in Rockefeller Center in 1935.

At first glance, Wright's vision of the good life seems refreshing and enlightened. Each citizen would have had a one-acre parcel of land on which to raise family crops, enjoy nature, and find the solitude impossible in the clash of city life. Landscaped highways, free of billboards and stop signs, were never far. The modern railroad and Wright's favorite toy, the car, made a more mobile and decentralized life possible, connecting citizens with cultural centers for symphonies, theaters, and art museums set in their own natural expanses. Shopping and businesses were reached by a highway system that leaped over local byways on overpasses. Even more distant natural attractions were within reach: Wright envisioned private airplanes and the yet-to-be-invented helicopter as common transit. Lovely. But illusory.

Broadacre City was never a possibility. If one acre had been given to each family, this "natural" environment would have gobbled all the land available. Wright's doll-like utopia on a flat plywood base was orderly and sweet, but it didn't take notice of the disorderliness of real land, real villages, real people, and real economic forces.

A disturbing ghost lurks behind the noble Broadacre concept.

How could a government actually create such a uniform, harmonious, and endlessly boring succession of tiny private farms? Only a totalitarian government with absolute powers over its citizens could force a large population into a rigid structure. Who would dictate the design and management of this decentralized idyll? In Wright's mind, of course, the architect would be the fascist leader.

Wright's arguments sounded like the wholesome advice of a farmer: "Get out of the evil city!" He showed contempt for the "vainglorious skyscraper," even though he was quite willing to design them himself. But Wright was no earthy farmer. What we can hear in the advice is Wright's refusal to struggle with complex problems. A city grows for a reason and has its own vitality, but thorny social and physical problems come with the energy and usefulness of a city. Wright had no practical solution beyond running away.

Broadacre exists today in a corrupt and disturbing form. We call it "suburbia," the 'burbs. Almost the entire length of the Eastern Seaboard and great tracts of land inland are occupied by an endless "megalopolis." This is a super-city composed of suburbs that have spread helter-skelter from city centers to join in one giant suburb. Unplanned batches of housing developments, strip malls, shopping centers, and tangled streets stretch for hundreds of miles.

Broadacre principles apply to these suburban homes in twisted ways. Each family occupies its parcel of land outside the city (usually only a fraction of an acre). Each house is separated from the next by local zoning laws that specify "setbacks" from the property lines. Each community of ranch houses (a curious title) is connected to schools, businesses, shopping, and cultural opportunities just as Broadacre City was—by a miraculous system of superhighways.

The utopian dream of Broadacre—or something very like it—created a living monster. Highway-linked suburban shopping centers drain commerce from nearby cities. City centers lose income and fall into disrepair. Crime and poverty become inevitable. The utopian cure has been the cause.

Wright refused to recognize that Broadacre City would handcuff American life to more cars and more oil, forever. As our population increases, the supply of oil declines, gas prices rise, and unstable nations control the access to oil, Broadacre City has become a deepening nightmare.

Remnants of other social engineering exist, like Le Corbusier's models of workers' housing grouped in a pleasant park environment. We call them "the projects," utopian city attempts to give low-cost housing to low-income families. They have become bitter, crime-infested battlegrounds.

There is a deeper flaw at the very core of the Broadacre concept. Society is a cooperative project. Decentralized, far-flung, quietly solitary Broadacre did away with neighborhoods, perhaps the most important part of society. Cities can be messy, but they are not necessarily evil cancers. Cities have a real function: a concentration of people encourages connection. The city makes sharing ideas, friendship, business, and communication a little easier. Neighborhoods are where we learn to get along, to meet by chance, to agree and disagree—not long distance, not by appointment, but by being close.

Wright was a brilliant designer but almost pathetically naïve in political belief.

In spite of their blatant fascism and militarism, Wright continued to hold fond thoughts of Germany and Japan. Their recognition of his genius softened his view of their racist, predatory actions.

He even accepted an invitation from the First All-Union Congress of Soviet Architects and traveled to Moscow in 1937. Olgivanna translated for him in her native language. The *Autobiography* reports thunderous applause, but he was only politely received by the politically sophisticated and ideologically cautious Soviet architects (free thinking and reckless talk led to liquidation under Stalin). They recognized him as a thinly disguised aristocrat. A few difficult experiences in the U.S.S.R. convinced him that his own "mobocracy" was kinder and more receptive to revolutionaries than communism.

Wright was whimsical and inconsistent—we might say "illogical"—in his political beliefs. He supported Franklin Delano Roosevelt in his social reforms to end the Depression and reassure Americans. He objected, however, to Roosevelt's desire to help Britain or any other nation against Nazi Germany, aggressive militaristic Japan, Stalin's U.S.S.R. (allied, at first, with

Hitler), or fascist Italy. Why should any world conflict affect life at Taliesin?

Nearing seventy, Frank Lloyd Wright saw himself grandly as a world citizen beyond nationality. He believed that he was a man of the future. Broadacre was his preciously miniature vision of the bright promise in future life. He felt he was above the old warning, "Beware of what you wish for; you may get it."

• 18 •

USONIA

ONE OF THE building blocks for Broadacre City was well-designed, affordable housing for every family. Though he was famous for his home commissions for the wealthy, and infamous for his cost overruns, Wright still struggled with the ideal of sensible and gracious living in a small space, cheaply built. He even coined a word for these kinds of houses: he called them *Usonian homes*. Perhaps he was playing on a European abbreviation for the United States—USoNA, United States of North America. Perhaps he was combining "utopian" and "U.S."

The Usonian homes were a development of his Prairie Style, refined and downscaled to fit modest budgets, and he devoted serious time to them. They were designed according to Wright's belief that a vast space was not necessary for a spacious feeling. How the inner space was manipulated made that feeling, and this was one of Wright's great talents. He reached for two competing but desirable virtues: the warm, protected sense of shelter, and the open, light-filled sense of elbow room. He achieved this by shaping the zones of the home without confining walls, and by using stretches of continuous floor and ceiling to bind the parts. There were three zones: the living zone; a joined kitchen and dining zone; a sleeping and bath zone. Of these, only the bath and bedrooms were set apart by walls.

The kitchen, which he called the "work area," flowed easily into the dining area. This was an innovation: most kitchens were considered "utility" areas, not fit for guests to see. Often kitchens were the domain of a servant, but Wright designed the Usonian homes for young couples of modest income and made no provisions for servants. He was designing a new, more honest, more sensible kind of living within a new kind of house. (He didn't practice this kind of living, but he preached it well.) This openness changed American architecture, because the kitchen in a Usonian home was exposed. It needed to be as well finished and attractive as the rest of the home.

The dining area flowed into the living area with some graceful hesitation—perhaps a right angle in an L-shaped plan, perhaps a peekaboo screen, perhaps only a change in floor or ceiling level to delineate the zones. The living area was the social focus of the home and held the inevitable Wright fireplace.

The plans of Usonian homes were modular, usually built on squares or rectangles, though Wright tried hexagons, octagons, and triangles. Arranging geometry like this was familiar to the old Froebel playmate, but this consistency of measures also organized the building, oriented the inhabitants, and made construction easier. There was a masonry core at the juncture of zones where Wright clustered the "mechanicals"—the plumbing, large appliances for heating and laundry, all the "services" of a home. Putting them together was convenient for plumbers and electricians and saved money.

Most Usonian homes were a single story and incorporated Wright's customary insistence on privacy.

They usually presented a private side to the street with few or no windows, but opened easily with many windows or whole window walls to the private terrace and garden behind the house. This "family side" of the house was oriented toward the south, to welcome light.

The general lines of the house were horizontal, a logical development of the Prairie Style homes, most often with flat roofs reaching well beyond the walls in calculated overhangs that blocked the high, hot summer sun but admitted low winter sun and natural surrounding light. The horizontal lines were emphasized by the use of horizontal wood siding, laid stone, or brick. The materials were natural and honest, local if possible. Wood was stained rather than painted, to preserve the grain; brick was a natural color. Wright stressed an inside/outside flow, a look of continuity, by using the same materials and finishes inside and out.

These homes were built without garages but acknowledged the importance of the car with a roof extension that formed a weather-sheltering carport (Wright may have invented the name). They had no attics and no basements, though furnaces, hot-water heaters, and laundry appliances were sometimes lowered into small sub-levels.

The Usonian houses were showcases of Wright's design genius. These small cottages surprised visitors with their warmth, sense of space, and new ideas.

Wright dispensed with the radiator and fell back on a system of heating the floor, taking advantage of hot air's natural tendency to rise and heat the whole space. He laid hot-water heating pipes in gravel beneath the concrete surface. This "radiant" heat rose from a warm, comforting floor.

To save money and to impress a consistent design theme on each home, much of the furniture was built in—bookshelves, counters, sofas, cabinets, and tables. In a few homes Wright offered simple plywood furniture, somewhat improved from his early vicious furniture. Plywood in furniture, walls, ceilings, and floors was a Wright favorite: it was stable, strong, utilized more of the tree, and could be beautiful when used well.

Textiles in the homes, chosen by Wright, were robust and textural in earth tones, almost never in a pattern. Wright believed that patterned upholstery and curtains confused the balance of a room's elements. When a pattern did appear—perhaps in a Navajo rug or a Persian carpet—the break with planes and solid colors made them more interesting.

The great quality of a Usonian home—of any Wright home—was that no aspect of floor, wall, ceiling, door, window, texture, or color had been overlooked as an opportunity to achieve beauty. A common reaction after visiting a Wright home—even a tiny Usonian gem built on a tiny budget—is disappointment in the homes most of us occupy. In the Wright creation we see a wholly designed home, built around a well-thought-out concept to make an artistic and useful statement.

The Hannas, Paul and Jean, had visited Taliesin in 1931. In 1935 Paul was invited to join the faculty of Stanford University in Palo Alto, California. They asked Wright to design a house for them and their three children on a modest budget.

With Wright, they wrote a program for the home, setting out what they wanted it to accomplish. They spelled out what kind of spaces they wanted for study, entertaining, family, cooking, outdoor living. They made the feeling of the house part of the program, and how it should help them achieve a better life. The Hannas were good clients. When Wright brought in some strange notion that wasn't part of the program, they refused. They rejected his built-in beds only thirty inches wide and insisted on a standard mattress size. They wouldn't have halls less than twenty inches wide; they wanted to walk down halls without scraping their elbows. There was some shouting, many hot letters, but eventual harmony. The result was small, efficient, and unusual. The module was a hexagon, like the cell of a honeycomb. Like a bee colony, the plan folded and wrapped around itself. The Hannas' budget was $15,000, but the first building estimates came in at $20,000. The special angles and unconventional methods cost the builders more time than expected. The cost estimates went up to $25,000. Before the house was complete, the costs had risen to $37,000.

The process was long, uncomfortable, occasionally angry, and worth the effort on both sides. The Hannas and their children lived in the house for many years. In the fifties, they were brave enough to ask Wright for additions—a guesthouse and a workshop. They finally deeded the house to Stanford University as one of the jewels of American domestic architecture. After their long wrangle with Wright, the Hannas said their home was "the loveliest shelter we have ever seen."

Herbert and Katherine Jacobs were also good Wright clients, for a different reason: they were innocents. They had one daughter and close to no money, but they wanted a wonderful house. Herbert presented himself at Taliesin and confessed to a budget of only $5,000. Could Wright design a home for them with that? Their simple trust in Wright was irresistible. In some way, the old con man was conned.

Their budget was really $4,500, he told them, because he had to charge $500 for designing it.

They had less than that, because they owned no land and had to scrape together $800 for a small lot in Madison.

Disaster! The Federal Home Administration, on which they had counted for a low-cost home loan, wouldn't finance a house with an unconventional flat roof. They couldn't borrow the money. By chance a local banker had spent many happy evenings in Wright's Midway Gardens and wrote them a mortgage.

The tiny home, less than 1,500 square feet, was to be built in three months of the summer, but it eventually took twelve months to complete. It was magical in the illusion it created: it looked small from outside, but twice as big inside! Typically Usonian, it presented an almost blind wall to the street, relieved by high, light-gathering windows. The front door was a puzzle to find. But on the other side of Wright's privacy barrier, it opened to a private garden from every room toward the south.

Predictably, it broke the Jacobses' budget, eventually costing $20,000.

Like many Wright buildings, it was famous before it was even finished. Constantly interrupted by sightseers, the Jacobs charged twenty-five cents for a tour. When *Architectural Forum* brought out an all-Wright issue featuring the house, they had to raise the price to fifty cents.

The famous architect Walter Gropius, recently immigrated from Vienna, came to marvel at the little wonder on a rainy day. Wright, still scornful of the modernist "jackals," wouldn't meet him for a tour. Apparently he paid his fifty cents like everyone else.

Like every other Wright home, the Jacobs house leaked badly. Katherine Lloyd Jones, the wife of Wright's cousin, lived in another Wright home. During a rainstorm, she looked up at her guests as she shuffled pots under the leaks from her Wright roof and said, "Well, this is what we get for leaving a work of art out in the rain."

The Usonian "style" was not a phase or a brief interlude. Between 1930 and his death in 1959, Frank Lloyd Wright created 140 Usonian homes. He had created an American icon, a beautifully simple idea of a working, sheltering, harmonious homeplace.

The difficulty and danger of beautiful ideas is that they can become ugly and destructive in the wrong hands and at the wrong time.

The generalities of the Usonian concepts were seized by speculators and developers and corrupted by the same market forces Wright had worked against for more than forty years. Pretence, mindless decoration, outworn building methods, and greed changed the light and graceful Usonian home into the monster ranch house that galloped across the country, devouring land. Developers discovered it was easy to build a flat-roofed, one-story home with a carport. It was not easy to duplicate Wright's playful manipulation of space and texture. Builders added cheap, pre-made mantles to brick veneer fireplaces. They walled off the kitchen and the dining room as conventional boxes with standard openings for doors and windows. Why? Because builders worked in ways they knew with materials they knew. These un-Wright, partly Usonian houses sold because buyers were accustomed to living in boxes. They'd never lived in a Wright home.

In some ways, you probably live in a Wright home. Wright's influence is inescapable. If your kitchen flows into your dining room, if your house is arranged in zones, if you have sliding-glass doors or window walls leading onto a terrace where you barbecue and sit in the summer, Wright has touched your life.

• 19 •

STREAMLINING

IN THE YEARS between World Wars, science inspired art. The cause was simple: speed. With high-speed cars, airplanes, and fast steam locomotives, humans were moving at greater speeds, fast enough that simple air resistance was becoming a more important factor. The shapes of fast-moving objects were "streamlined," smoothed and simplified to reduce the resistance.

Streamlining was applied to airplanes, certainly, but streamlined shapes became popular for everything, even objects that didn't move, like kitchen mixers, toasters, and pencil sharpeners. The flow over surfaces was emphasized by parallel "streamlines" that became a rhythmic theme of the style.

Shining metal echoed the modern materials of airplanes and cars. Electric lights were also a factor in the new art, so translucent or transparent glass and plastic played a central part. Machine-generated arcs and shapes combined with this exuberant rush toward the future and resulted in a style we now call Art Deco.

Frank Lloyd Wright was affected by this rush to the future and was enthusiastic about streamlining. He was looking for a way to reflect the spirit of modern mobility, rapid movement, and powerful vitality in his architecture. To express this new concept in architecture, he needed a new client, a new pigeon to pluck.

Wright's next pigeon was tougher and more formidable than the rest, and Wright would make millions of dollars out of his company.

Herbert F. "Hib" Johnson's grandfather had founded the Johnson Wax Company in Racine, Wisconsin. In 1935 it was one of the largest and wealthiest privately owned companies. It manufactured waxes and paints, necessities for maintaining buildings, which sold well right through the Depression. The company remained solid.

Hib Johnson was in his thirties, intelligent, artistic, and quietly, politely stubborn. His company needed a new corporate headquarters. Like the executives of the Larkin Company, he considered the company's employees a "family." He was disappointed in conventional designs with Roman arches and niches for statuary.

His general manager, Jack Ramsey, had visited Taliesin and raved about the architecture and the architect. Johnson visited Wright. The old fox pretended not to be interested but had his apprentices cleaning and preparing Taliesin for days.

Johnson appeared with a load of doubt. Wright hadn't lived down his old reputation. Racine had only one Wright home, attractive in itself but uncomfortable in its setting of conventional homes. Hib Johnson was prepared to regard Wright as an oddball.

It was a terrible visit. They began arguing within half an hour of Johnson's arrival and snapped at each other right through dinner. They insulted each other and disagreed on every subject. Johnson was half Wright's age, yet they butted heads like schoolboys on the same playground. They agreed on only one thing: they both owned Lincoln Zephyrs.

Wright had an uncanny sense of seduction. He knew when to flatter, and when to insult.

When Johnson returned to Racine, he sent Wright a letter proposing that he design the Johnson Wax corporate headquarters with a budget of $200,000 and an architect's commission of 10 percent. He enclosed a check for $1,000 to bind the deal.

Some biographers have called Frank Lloyd Wright the greatest "snake-oil salesman" ever. But he built up complex relationships with some clients that lasted many years. With Hib Johnson, Wright sometimes acted like a father and sometimes like a rascally younger brother.

Wright immediately went beyond his commission. He told Johnson that the city was dead and he must take his company and its employees into the broad countryside to build a new town on Wright's principles. He pressed hard for weeks. Johnson and his people resisted firmly.

Olgivanna demonstrated her power over the master's temper and stubborn notions. "Give them what they want, Frank, or you will lose the job." He relented and began to design.

He shook an astonishing and entirely new concept out of his sleeve. The design for a new era in corporate architecture took ten days. He proposed to build and furnish it for $250,000 within one year.

The contractor chosen was cautious about building one of the Wright's infamous designs. He knew about Wright's constant changes and untried construction methods. He agreed to build the corporate center for the actual cost of construction plus a set percentage.

The building was like nothing anyone had ever seen, but it followed many of the principles Wright had developed for the Larkin Company offices. One was an almost religious regard for work. A favorite saying of Wright's hung in his own drafting room at Taliesin: *"As a man does, a man is."* This came as close to a plain religious creed as Wright got. For him the workplace was a kind of temple to energy, ingenuity, and activity. For Johnson Wax he wanted to create another temple of work, glowing with light, removed from outside pollutants and distractions, an enclosed and sheltering place in which employees could work happily. He succeeded.

Like Unity Temple, the Johnson Wax Center was a grouping of three elements: a great workspace, an annex, and a connecting corridor that held the entrance.

The Johnson Wax Center in Racine, Wisconsin.

Unlike the Unity Temple's stern, spare rectangles and squares, the exterior form of the buildings was streamlined, all curve and swoop.

Wright played on the theme of squares and circles to create rhythms and patterns everywhere, and everywhere the smooth horizontal streamlining was apparent in the near-complete absence of hard corners. Walls met one another in a smooth curve. The exterior was buff-colored brick with a horizontal band of marvelous glass. It rose toward the roof but stopped short. The roof seemed to float without contact to the solid walls.

The strange glass was a Wright invention that never quite worked. The "light bands" were an outer and inner stack of glass tubes. They were wired into place on internal aluminum racks. Between the stacks of tubes, electric lights provided a consistent level of illumination as darkness fell. They weren't "windows"—there was no view through the tubes. The light bands and the texture of the parallel tubes were part of the streamlined flow. They gave an unusually pleasant quality of light within.

The walls were another Wright invention. They weren't massive masonry but two relatively thin layers of brick supported and insulated by light cork between them.

The grandest and most impressive space—the large rectangular work area in the office building—was about 220 feet by 120 feet, on a 20-foot-square module. A brick *mezzanine* (a raised "half floor") ran around the exterior walls, with offices opening to its interior walkway. The vast space would be an artificial forest of delicate, graceful columns inspired by trees. They were a radical new design made of hollow reinforced concrete only 9 inches in diameter at their bronze sockets on the floor. The main columns rose to about 18 feet, then spread out from a transitional "collar" to a disk 18 feet, 6 inches across. Each column would be set in place on a bronze floor post, and secured to its neighboring column-disks by steel connectors. Between the columns was a four-pointed shape, and above these spaces were "tents" of the same glass tubes.

At this point, plans for the Johnson Wax Center slammed to a halt. The Wisconsin State Building Code had structural rules about the height and thickness of columns. For the height and the amount of roof area each *dendriform* (treelike) column proposed to support, the code called for a column diameter of 30 inches. Nine inches was ridiculous. They couldn't issue a building permit for anything so flimsy.

In the dispute over the columns it was also discovered that Frank Lloyd Wright, at seventy, had never been issued a license to practice architecture. The state was obliging in this matter and granted a "special" license to the most famous architect in the world.

But the columns simply wouldn't work.

Wright cheerfully suggested that they try one column and see if it would support the weight. He had faith in his intuitive engineering design sense.

A test was arranged. A single dendriform column was built to Wright's specifications. On June 4, 1937, only one week after the column's concrete had been poured and even before it had reached its full strength, it was set up in a field. Since the "forest" of columns would support one another, wooden beams braced the column against wobbling. Predictably, Wright had summoned the press. Wright, "the boys," Hib Johnson, and the contractor for the project stood about with reporters and photographers. Only Wright seemed enthusiastic. Upwards of a hundred people had come to see the column fail.

In midmorning a crane began to load the graceful disk with bags of sand. To be certified by the building code, it had to hold 12 tons. The bags were lifted and counted.

By noon the load had reached 12 tons and the state

inspectors declared that they were satisfied. Wright said, "Keep going!"

By midafternoon there were no more sandbags, and the load on the slim column had reached 30 tons. Wright said, "Keep piling!" and a supply of much heavier pig iron was hoisted up onto the disk. In the late afternoon there was no more weight to hoist. The column was holding 60 tons with no sign of distress. Everyone wanted to go home. Wright agreed, and had one of the wooden side-props pulled out. The column and its enormous load came crashing down. Even then, the column didn't break.

Later technical analysis of the hollow, thin-wall dendriform columns showed that Wright had accurately directed all the forces to flow along the curve from upper disc to ground post perfectly. He had devised something fresh in engineering, a thin-shelled structure that held its stress at the surface. It opened a new world of possibilities that other engineers and architects are still exploring.

Building on the Johnson Wax Center began.

The contractor's cost-plus contract was a wise precaution. The Johnson Wax Center required three years and $3,000,000 to build. In 1939 this expense was immense, shocking. Johnson Wax, because it was wealthy and privately owned, was perhaps the only company in the United States that could have completed the project.

On the plus side, Johnson Wax had received millions of dollars in free publicity. Once again Wright had designed an icon of the time. It appeared all over the world in every architectural journal, every major newspaper. There was no building remotely like it. It was a new architectural and artistic statement about the corporate world and work.

The quality of light from Wright's glass-tube "windows" was nothing less than magic. It really was a "temple of work," but it was also fun, exciting, energizing.

Hib Johnson was delighted about the way the center made Johnson Wax employees feel, but there were a few items on the minus side beside being $2,750,000 over budget. There was the furniture. The typically vicious Wright three-legged chairs dumped many employees on the floor before they were replaced with conventional four-legged chairs.

The glass tubes brought in beautiful light, but they also let the rain come in by the bucketful. Wright tried to find a way to seal the space between tubes—strips of rubber and dozens of caulking mixtures. Nothing ever worked. The center leaked for years. Eventually, a new and conventionally waterproof roof had to be built over the sieve-like Wright roof and special lights installed above the glass tubes to provide the illusion of daylight. Many years later, the wall bands of Pyrex were removed entirely and substituted by thick glass specially cast to look like the original tubes.

In 1944, at the height of World War II, Johnson must have forgotten all the strains of working with Wright, because he asked him to design a research tower beside the original enter. Wright was delighted because he had originally planned the Johnson Wax Center to have a matching vertical element.

Wright approached tower building in a fresh way, sinking a deep "tap root" foundation at the center as the basis of a stiff, strong core. His floors were cantilevered out from the core. Replacing heavy load-bearing walls on the exterior were lightweight, light-transmitting walls. He used the same glass tubing in deeper bands separated by bands of the lightweight brick and cork sandwich. Inside the glass, dimly visible as a shape from the outside, was the cylindrical core with elevators and stairs.

He called it a Heliolab because it welcomed a full day of natural sunlight. It was elegant. During the day, light reflected from the tubes like a torch. During the night, the tower's interior lighting made a beacon of light.

Beautiful it is. Striking and fascinating, even today. But it didn't work. Of course it leaked, but everyone expected that. Sunlight lancing through the Pyrex made it too bright for work without shades over desks and counters. It also pushed the temperature to unbearable levels, and even massive air-conditioning units couldn't keep up with the heat. During the Wisconsin winter, the leaky Pyrex tubes bled expensive heat. Wright refused to install an "ugly" sprinkler system, so the fire hazard prevented any real laboratory work. Tiny stairwells out of proportion to the occupancy made it useless as an office building. The beautiful, shining beacon was quietly abandoned except for tour groups of admiring visitors. There have been many attempts to make it useful to Johnson Wax as more than a symbol, but no solutions have been successful yet.

The American Institute of Architects kept its distance from Frank Lloyd Wright through much of his lifetime. His methods and finances were questionable, and he criticized his fellow architects too wickedly. But at length it recognized the Johnson Wax Center as one of the significant architectural gifts to American culture. Some say that it is the finest corporate workplace ever built. Some say that it is among the very finest pieces of American art.

• 20 •

TIME TRAVELING

MOST IDEAS ARRIVE just in time. They solve immediate problems or leap out of new needs. But a few ideas have arrived before society was prepared for them.

Frank Lloyd Wright was a geyser of new ideas. They came gushing out of him. They were always brilliant, even the failures. A few of his designs were anachronisms, ideas ahead of or behind their time. Wright never threw away an idea that had some valuable part. If it didn't work for this project, it would work for another. He kept thousands of schemes in the "not yet" drawer of his designer's mind. The file drawers of Taliesin hold incomplete projects that are also precious resources of intellect. The hundreds of unbuilt designs still witness his mastery of architecture.

Wright was once asked by a television mogul if he could design a broadcasting tower of several hundred feet. Wright asked why the executive was so timid? Why not go a mile? And so he designed The Illinois, a mile-high skyscraper of extraordinary beauty, obvious genius, and practical engineering. It will never be built, but is nevertheless a wonder. The concept even impressed Wright, who made the original rendering twenty-three feet high, a work of art in itself.

Another idea ahead of its time was the Jacobs Solar Hemicycle. Before the energy crisis, before the price of oil skyrocketed and heating was a major part of home expenses, Wright created one of the first solar homes. It was energy efficient before society began to ask for efficient use of energy.

The form of the house was shaped by the arc of the sun's transit through the southern sky. In the winter, the arc tilts lower and every moment of solar warmth is precious in the bitter Wisconsin climate. In the summer, the arc climbs higher in the sky, and heat is more of a foe than a friend. Wright shaped the glass-fronted home as a southern-facing curve that welcomed the winter sun through the day. For when the arc climbed, however, Wright provided a precisely calculated shade, an "eyebrow" that would block out direct sunlight between a day in late spring and another in early autumn. In the hollow of the house's concave curve, a sunken garden absorbed the sunlight. Wright designed a pool that passed under the glass of the living area, used by the Jacobs for beauty in the winter, and refreshing plunges in the summer. The convex north side of the curve was a wall built of concrete and stone, a fortification against wind and cold, most of it covered by an angled earth berm.

Always playing peekaboo and juggling opposites, Wright designed the Solar Hemicycle to look like an arms-open gallery from the south, and like a castle fortress from the north. As a mechanism, as an essay in engineering, and as a home, the Hemicycle shone; it was form and function.

In 1939 Wright was offered the largest and most complete project of his career, a complex of enormous size to be built on the last undeveloped parcel of wooded land in downtown Washington, D.C.: fifteen acres at the juncture of Connecticut and Florida Avenues. The projected costs of the project, Crystal Heights, were estimated at ten to fifteen million dollars. It was to be the pinnacle of his professional life and, as a major feature of the nation's capital, only half a mile north of the White House, an affirmation of his place in American art.

What Wright shook out of his sleeve was a practical work of mature genius, a composition of white marble towers on an enormous triangular plaza, perched on the shoulder of the slope toward the Potomac. The multi-use towers were to hold 2,500 hotel and apartment rooms, a cinema, restaurants, shops, and, beneath the plaza, five stories of parking.

The tallest tower was designed at 135 feet, slightly over the District's height restrictions for the site. A routine *code variance*—special permission for special cases—was necessary. The variance was denied.

The syndicate of financial backers was furious, but not as vocal and biting as Wright. He damned the National Capital Park and Planning Commission for clinging to the outworn Greek and Roman styles that made up every public building downtown.

The chairman of the National Capital Park and

Planning Commission was Frederic A. Delano, an admiring advocate of the Beaux Arts tradition. With the backing of every traditional architect in the District of Columbia, Maryland, and Virginia, the commission announced its immovable opposition to the Crystal Heights project. The financial backers withdrew their support. Wright returned to Taliesin West to fume and recuperate. A setback of this size would be hard on a young man, but for a man of seventy-three it must have been overwhelming.

Frank Lloyd Wright knew that his work would outlast him and all of the people who criticized him. In one sense, he was a time-traveler, designing for another age.

• 21 •

AN ECLIPSE OF THE SUN

AN OLD PROVERB says, "God loves a fool." Wright was a brilliant designer and engineer, but as a political activist he was a fool.

Almost everyone saw World War II coming. Almost everyone tried to believe it could be avoided. In hindsight we can see that a violent showdown between the fascist nations and the liberal nations was inevitable.

The goals of Hitler's Germany were apparent to anyone who listened: a commanding position in world affairs, retribution for the humiliation of Germany at the end of World War I, racial purity, and more territory.

Fascist Italy was a strong ally of Germany under Il

Duce, Benito Mussolini, who fell in with Hitler's principles. Japan was dominated by a fanatically militaristic brotherhood who believed Japan's destiny was to rule the Pacific Ocean.

In 1938 Germany took over the German-speaking country of Austria without much fuss. Later that year it invaded the Sudetenland, a largely German-speaking section of Czechoslovakia. In September of 1939 a squadron of bombers crossed into Polish airspace and bombed bridges and military outposts just ahead of invading German troops. The *blitzkrieg* ("lightning war") was on.

France and Britain had no alternative to declaring war and hoping Hitler would back down. A few days later most of Europe was at war.

After Hitler's troops overran Poland, France, Belgium, Holland, Norway, Denmark, and North Africa, there was no doubt that a struggle between dictatorship and democracy, between totalitarian darkness and liberal light, had arrived.

There is a puzzle no one has ever solved: Why do very smart people do such dumb things?

Frank Lloyd Wright saw all these things happen, heard all the details, but threw them aside as unimportant. He loved the German people because they loved him. Would they do wicked things? Never.

More important events were happening! He had survived the Great Depression and had returned to his position as the most famous American architect. The Johnson Wax Center had encouraged dozens of new commissions. The Taliesin Fellowship was booming. He had Taliesin North in Spring Green and Taliesin West near Phoenix. He had a record number of new apprentices and, suddenly, he was recognized as a creative genius by the world.

Wright insisted that the struggle in Europe didn't concern him.

In January of 1938, *Architectural Forum* had published an all-Wright issue. Later that year he was on the cover of *Time* magazine, and one of his designs was on the cover of *Life* magazine. He was made a member of the American Academy of Arts and Letters in the United States, and the Academies of Arts in Mexico and Uruguay. He was invited to lecture at the Royal Institute of British Architects in London, and was awarded their Royal Gold Medal for architecture.

His old adversary, the Museum of Modern Art, had reconsidered the bare, cold International Style (which, Wright claimed, was grounded in his work) and pronounced it dated and dead. In 1940, MoMA announced a large exhibit of Wright's work. The critic Lewis Mumford called him "undoubtedly the world's greatest living architect, a man who can dance circles around any of his contemporaries."

He had charmed the world and seemed to have all the glory and adulation he had wanted. Now a shadow passed over his glory, the same shadow of war that was passing over every nation, and it infuriated Wright. He objected to the war. It would affect his work, his life, his security.

Frank Lloyd Wright called himself a pacifist. He was fond of saying, "War solves nothing." He threw up a wordy smokescreen, talking about noble pacifist ideas, but his central concern seemed apparent: war would slow down or simply stop new building.

Always anti-British, he insisted that the entire mess was Britain's fault. The three foreign nations he loved were Germany, Italy, and Japan. Wright called the nations who were fighting them "gangsters" and lumped President Franklin Delano Roosevelt in with them. The press, always eager for Wright copy, printed his inflammatory sentiments.

He was unbelievably out of touch in an era of intense national crisis. He insisted that he and his apprentices were not Americans but international artists. They owed no allegiance to petty nations. Indeed, he called for an end to nations and borders as "obsolete."

Wright lent his famous voice to an isolationist movement called America First with his friend Charles A. Lindberg. Its announced purpose was to keep America out of a European war. Though some of the intellectual spokesmen, like Lindberg, were honorable, there was a deeper, bigoted faction and distinct pro-German involvement.

Wright's frequent statements raised eyebrows at the FBI. Director J. Edgar Hoover considered Wright dangerous. He reopened Wright's FBI file from the time of his divorce and began investigating him for the serious charge of sedition.

Around this time the concept of the Fellowship

was put to a serious test. Edgar Tafel was one of the senior members of the Fellowship and one of Wright's most trusted assistants for many years. He wanted to design his own buildings within the framework of the Fellowship as a full architect rather than an assistant to Wright. He offered to split his fees with the Fellowship. Wright offered him an insulting one-third of any fee. Trying hard to make a shift in the way the Fellowship worked, Tafel brought a commission into the drafting room. Wright ignored Tafel's work and never paid him his share of the fee. Disillusioned and disappointed, Tafel and six other senior apprentices left Wright and Taliesin forever.

In 1941 Japan attacked American bases all over the Pacific, most notably at Pearl Harbor in Hawaii. A few days later, Germany and Italy joined in a declaration of war on America, and the United States was a part of the worldwide struggle. A draft of all young men was ordered.

Wright fought to retain his apprentices and their services. He appealed to the government in Washington for a special exemption on the grounds that the

Taliesin Fellowship was involved in artistic work that would be critical to the country when the war was over. The request was denied. Wright appealed to the local draft board for an exemption on the grounds that Taliesin was a working farm and his apprentices were needed to keep it running. This might have worked, but he included a twenty-five-page letter criticizing the government, questioning the need for war, accusing political leaders of aiding Britain to keep its ailing Empire, and so on. No exemption.

Wright suggested that his apprentices register as conscientious objectors, a status reserved for long-standing religious groups whose traditional doctrines forbade serving in armed forces (like the Society of Friends, sometimes called Quakers). Though Taliesin was run like a cult, it had no religious affiliation. Conscientious objector status was not granted, and several apprentices were imprisoned.

A local federal judge heard the conscientious objector case of one apprentice and concluded, logically, that Wright had counseled the young men to resist the draft. He ordered the FBI to investigate. Hoover asked the Justice Department to file an indictment, but the department declined to bring charges. It's difficult to understand why. Perhaps fame shielded Wright. Perhaps the Justice Department simply recognized that he was a brilliant artist but a bit of a crackpot and, though loud and peevish, essentially harmless.

Was Wright a Nazi? Was he a Communist?

He wasn't nearly politically perceptive enough to be either. His philosophy was more noise than sense. It was the extravagant pulpit talk of a born preacher that didn't allow logic to clutter his grandiloquent phrases. He never looked at the hard facts.

Was he, like Hitler, anti-Semitic?

It's true that Wright had used some nasty racial slurs to describe Jews, but he'd slurred almost every sector of society at one time or another. Many of Wright's apprentices, clients, and benefactors, including Fallingwater's Kaufmann, were Jews. He was carelessly offensive but not anti-Semitic.

By the time World War II came to an end, Wright had effectively alienated himself from the press and the people of the country.

For a few years his brightness was eclipsed by the

war and by the resentment of the American people at his loudly unpatriotic views. But one of the virtues of a large, liberal society is that we forgive easily and without much rancor. When the dark time was over, Wright shone again.

• 22 •

A MYSTIC SPIRAL

SOLOMON R. GUGGENHEIM was born into a family of plungers, aggressive businessmen who bought and sold for high stakes during the wide-open expansion of late-nineteenth-century America. This was the period of the "robber barons," and Solomon was one of the money pirates of his age. From an interest in two Colorado copper mines, the Guggenheims built a giant kingdom of money and influence. They battled the Rockefellers for almost complete control of metal mining and smelting in the United States. Solomon formed the Yukon Gold Company during the Alaskan gold rush, when the "Googlies" monopolized freight and ferry traffic between the United States and the Territory of Alaska. By 1920 the family had dominant interests in Bolivian tin, African diamonds, Chilean copper and nitrates (for fertilizer and gunpowder), Congolese rubber, Mexican chicle (for chewing gum), and copper, silver, and gold from Mexico and the United States.

In 1919, Solomon retired with more money than he could use and spent the rest of a long, sedate life collecting art.

In the late twenties, Mrs. Irene Guggenheim arranged for one of her favorite artists to paint her husband's portrait. It's a gentle study of an older man in knickerbockers (knee-britches) and plaid knee socks. While Solomon sat for the portrait, the artist spun a web of charm and fascination around him, not unlike the snares Frank Lloyd Wright spun for his fat pigeons.

The artist and charm-spinner was Baroness Hildegard Rebay von Ehrenwiesen, called Hilla Rebay. She was a modestly successful conventional artist but had manipulated her title and beauty to become a society contact and deal-maker for modern artists in the United States and Europe. She arranged meetings between the new artists and wealthy patrons, she brokered sales and became a patroness of new art.

Rebay convinced Solomon Guggenheim that old pictorial art was dead. To express real emotions, modern artists shouldn't be tied to paintings that looked like flowers or people or landscapes. Great art should be "non-objective," without an object-model in nature. She claimed that even abstraction—simplifying or interpreting parts of a subject as Picasso did in cubism or Matisse did in his figures—was not true art. The best new art should express emotions without likeness, with only shapes and colors and textures from the soul. The old robber-baron listened and became her patron, collecting works by Kandinsky, Klee, Bauer, Mondrian, and other non-objective artists. The artists he befriended and supported called him "Guggi."

His collection grew to represent the non-objective movement. When he recognized that his health was failing, he considered leaving his entire collection to the Metropolitan Museum of Art. But Guggenheim wanted his own museum. Many of his robber-baron friends—Freer, Frick, Huntington, Morgan, and Mellon—had built theirs. Rebay encouraged him to build a museum.

Who should design the museum? As in all artistic

matters, Guggenheim relied on Rebay's advice. International modernists were consulted: Le Corbusier, Walter Gropius, Mies van der Rohe, and others. But Rebay was convinced that "her" museum must be designed by an American architect in an American style. She mentioned a little sadly that Frank Lloyd Wright would be ideal if he were still alive.

Rebay was delighted to discover that Wright was not only still alive but eager to do new work. In the summer of 1943, Wright and Olgivanna arrived in New York and were put up at the Plaza Hotel overlooking Central Park, a creation of Frederick Law Olmstead, who had landscaped the White City for the Columbian Exposition of Wright's youth, long ago in 1893.

It's almost unnecessary to mention that Frank Lloyd Wright captivated Guggenheim and Rebay. Guggi was enraptured with the puckish, enthusiastic, but courtly figure. The old fox was small but more handsome than ever with his longish mane of white hair, his deep and melodious voice, his quick but fluid movement. Olgivanna, slim and beautiful with a bit of steel showing in her manner, made Wright even more appealing. They were a theatrical duo, an act that was hard to beat. The four of them became fast friends—though what friendship with clients was for Wright is a mystery.

Wright had no love for non-objective art, but he had few principles that could stand in the way of a fat commission. He was a man for all reasons, if a commission was available.

Another minor factor was that Wright had never designed a museum.

Wright received a contract for the Solomon R. Guggenheim Museum in 1943 with a budget of $750,000. It was a project he would work on for the rest of his life. The result would be another American icon. It became either an inspired and groundbreaking conception for a museum of art, or a monument to mismatched form and function. Critics, architects, and artists are still debating the outcome.

The form of the Guggenheim was preordained by Wright's prejudices.

Manhattan was, for Wright, the heart of the urban beast, a city he must "tame" to his conceptions. It was a rectilinear environment, all right angles and verticality. It was also a Beaux Arts city, with as many columns as ancient Rome and all the gewgaws of approved ornament so adored by the Paris school.

But New York also had a reputation for by-the-numbers practicality, get-it-done finality, and stock-market realism. It was a natural home to the International Style skyscraper: sheer walls of identical windows, like graph paper, rising to immense heights.

In the sixteen years Wright worked on the Guggenheim Museum's design and construction, many buildings rose in Manhattan, and Wright attacked all of them. Van der Rohe's giant, dark Seagram's Building stood across from the Skidmore, Owings and Merrill skyscraper, the Lever Building. Wright referred to this big American architecture firm as "Skidding Owe-More and Sterile," and named the facing buildings for their owner's products: "the whiskey building looking at the soap building." Over on the East River, the UN Buildings rose in the scored-block style—polished boxes of glass and metal without a concession to human scale or beauty. They were abstracts, disinfected shells, mathematical formulae.

To distinguish it from the styles Wright despised,

the Guggenheim Museum couldn't be rectilinear or classical in any visible way.

One of Wright's most cherished principles was that architecture should fit its site, not dominate it. A building should never be at the top of a hill but "of it." It's true that Wright had broken this basic precept of his architecture over and over, saying that the landscape was "improved" by his work. But a building's environment was a basic priority: site and structure should be in harmony. For the Guggenheim Museum, Wright discarded any consideration of surroundings or site. It's as if Wright meant to defy the city's fabric by planting an artifact from a completely different world on the Upper East Side of Manhattan.

Wright had played with the spiral for many years. It was one of nature's most intricate and magical forms— ever-expanding or ever-diminishing, each whorl in proportion to the whorl inside and outside it.

The first round of design for the Guggenheim Museum was a spiral that narrowed as it rose. The next design round was a hexagonal spiral of constant width.

The design process for almost any project and almost every art is iterative: it proceeds from a first idea

and goes through many stages of change and refine-
ment, or iterations. Most of Wright's designs went
through many iterations, though not all are recorded.
The Guggenheim was a public building with so much
public pressure on the outcome that a more complete
record was made of the progress from idea to idea.

It wasn't a smooth process.

It's difficult to know why, but Wright originally
wanted the exterior of the museum to be a bright red.
Then he suggested it be clad in bright reddish-pink
marble. Rebay vetoed this because red was, for her, a
crass and materialistic color.

Rebay and Guggenheim began to invite criticism of
the design from their architectural and artistic friends,
passing the advice on to Wright. It was Wright's turn
to veto. He made it clear that he was the designer and
that random suggestions didn't help, writing, "No great
and good thing in building ever happened where the
client was at the mercy of the passing suggestions of
this one and that one."

The design process dragged on. Real estate negotiations continued until the complete block at the
corner of Eighty-eighth Street and Fifth Avenue was

in Guggenheim's hands. Wright's budget estimate inevitably rose. From the original $750,000 it climbed to $1,500,000 and then to $2,500,000.

Construction should have begun soon after the war ended in 1945, but Guggenheim had a hunch that construction prices would go down, and so he held off. He waited too long.

Solomon R. Guggenheim died in 1949, leaving the Guggenheim Museum project in a perilous state. He left $2,000,000 for the construction of the museum and an additional $8,000,000 for the continuing care of the collection. There was no instruction in his will about the completion date of the museum, or even the specific architect who would finish the design. The trustees could have decided not to build the museum, and Wright could have been fired. Rebay was dismissed and a new, professional museum director was found. He questioned the actual worth of the collection, and doubted the worth of Wright's expensive building.

Luck was with the old fox again. Harry Guggenheim, Solomon's nephew and an admirer of Wright, took over the project and did his best to minimize the new budget's effects on architectural cutbacks.

Wright had another stroke of luck with Robert Moses, a cousin by marriage known to Wright as "Cousin Bob." Moses was a powerful figure in New York City politics. The design of the Guggenheim was radical, construction methods were unusual, and roadblocks of opposition rose from dozens of city committees, boards, inspectors, and officials. Their rules and codes didn't apply to massive concrete spirals. One legal problem was that the building rose outward, overhanging Fifth Avenue by over four feet! Moses was able to cut through the red tape to the archaic, corrupt heart of the city, so that construction began in the early fifties and continued for several years.

Contractors who bid on the job were accustomed to square corners and flat surfaces. The bids were astronomical. Edgar Tafel, the apprentice who was forced to leave Taliesin to express his own designs, helped Wright by acquainting him with a contractor who built highways and bridges. Rising curves and concrete construction were his bread and butter. His bid was more modest.

Wright never saw the Guggenheim finished in his

The Guggenheim Museum—exterior view.

lifetime, but it is one of the icons he left behind. It is a landmark, an indelible part of New York City's identity, and among the strangest architectural structures in the world.

Architecture is not a pure art. It never stands on its own but is always bound to its function, and to human scale. One measure of successful architecture is the way it works with people: do humans feel welcome in its setting? The Guggenheim Museum needed people. It invited visitors into its spaces. There were clues everywhere that this monumental, contemplative space was tailored to the human frame.

Wright created a sacred space for art. He also created an experience for the visitor. What is most important about the Guggenheim as Frank Lloyd Wright's creation is that it shapes our path, always insisting that *we are the flow*. We are the life of the spiral, revolving, rising, or falling to greet the paintings and sculpture on the path Wright gives us.

It is an almost mesmerizing space, and an unforgettable experience.

Is it a good museum?

It has inescapable problems. Its outward-sloping

walls are an uncomfortable plane on which to hang flat paintings, especially the very large paintings common today.

Another problem is hanging space. The architecture takes up so much room that the Guggenheim can't hang any great number of paintings.

Comfort is another problem. As visitors turn to face the paintings, they are on a downsloping ramp, right to left. Standing for long periods on even a slight angle can strain leg muscles.

The Solomon R. Guggenheim Museum didn't fit its city or its space. It didn't reflect the nature of nonobjective art or the purpose of a museum, and it didn't provide a great deal of space to view paintings. Once again, Wright expressed himself more than his subject or his clients. In these terms the Guggenheim is a "folly," an extravagant structure that is built for show, and stands for an idea more than a purpose. Some critics compared its round atrium with balconies to the tomb of Napoleon, and suggested that it was almost grandiose enough to make a tomb for Wright.

Frank Lloyd Wright, April 1959.

• 23 •

GLIDING HOME

THE GUGGENHEIM MUSEUM is usually listed as Wright's last great icon, but it was not the finest building of his last years. His small residences reflected his inventive genius more clearly.

The Taliesin Fellowship was thriving as Wright's personal design studio and fiefdom. After the war, hundreds of young men and women sought out the famous landmarks in Wisconsin or Arizona and asked to be part of the Fellowship. The best were accepted. They paid their hefty fees and entered what was almost a monastery: they lived a life of unquestioning service to the *lieber Meister* and the hazy ideals of the Fellowship. Their days were as closely managed as the holy hours of monks, and the dogma of Wright's beliefs was absolute. Heretical views were not encouraged.

The discipline and even personal life within the Fellowship were ruled more and more by Olgivanna. As Wright became older and more delicate, the Fellowship treated him more and more like a living saint.

Olgivanna was tough, blunt, and suspicious, but she had her vulnerabilities. During the war, the Fellowship had endured a special tragedy, one that scarred Olgivanna forever.

For many years, Wes Peters had been Wright's most trusted assistant. He was an engineer trained at MIT who found the Fellowship life calming and rewarding. Wright's only objection to the brilliant, handsome young man: at six-foot-five, he was too tall. Wright's ceilings were famously low and his sense of scale was formulated for his slight five-foot-six height. He would laughingly call out to Peters, "Sit down, Wes! You're ruining the scale!" In 1935 Wes Peters disobeyed Wright and Olgivanna and eloped with the daughter of her first marriage, Svetlana. Eventually the couple was forgiven and returned to the Fellowship. They became even more important in the life of the family, because Svetlana gave birth to two boys. In 1946 she was running errands in an open jeep with Brandoch, four years old, and Daniel, almost two, near Taliesin North. She was pregnant with their third child. The jeep swerved off a small bridge, somersaulted, and landed upside down in the stream below. Brandoch was thrown clear and ran up to the road, crying. Passing neighbors tried to help Svetlana and Daniel, but they both died in the crash. Olgivanna was destroyed by grief for months and mourned for years.

In a strange coincidence, Wes Peters married another Svetlana years later: Svetlana Alliluyeva, Josef Stalin's daughter.

Life at the Taliesins was not like the old potato soup days. In 1947 at least thirty-two commissions were on its drawing boards. The postwar building rush and Wright's revived fame were making it a successful studio. It was never more than Wright's tool, but the clannish Fellowship life created a smooth, energetic team that could churn out his projects quickly.

Wright was close to eighty, then, and kept up his phenomenal rush of ideas. At the Taliesins, he was often up at four in the morning, long before the apprentices. He worked quickly, with that uncanny ability to visualize everything on a flat sheet. He drew plans, elevations, and sections in different pencil colors, overlapping one another on the same sheet, to be redrawn on separate sheets by his apprentices. One morning he called "the boys" together as they entered the drafting room to redraw the dozens of individual sheets from his drawings; he had completed three separate designs that morning.

As the air of saintliness grew, he was less connected to "the boys." He and Olgivanna and their honored guests and clients now ate and listened to the evening entertainments on a raised platform, like royalty. He was absent from the drafting rooms for weeks, traveling more often.

In 1948 the American Institute of Architects, the organization and guild of professionals in the United States, finally awarded Frank Lloyd Wright their Gold Medal for achievement. If they expected him to have mellowed, they were wrong. His speech of acceptance was tart and critical of the state of architecture in America. In a way, they'd expected and perhaps even hoped for that.

There were three Taliesins now: Taliesin North in Spring Green, Wisconsin; Taliesin West, near

Phoenix, Arizona; and, informally, Taliesin East, a second-floor corner suite at the Plaza Hotel occupied by Wright as he spent more and more time in New York City. Wright was changing, becoming more of an urban figure, flashing about Manhattan with his red-lined cape and beret and cane. He was enjoying being what the public expected him to be—a rakish senior dissenter and a stylish curmudgeon. He was an honored guest at the best parties. He never passed up a chance to expound his views about architecture and art and everything else to newspaper, radio and television reporters.

Our image of the dashing architect is almost entirely Wright's invention. He was certainly one model for the most dramatic architect of fiction, Howard Roark in Ayn Rand's *The Fountainhead*.

In the last nine years of his extraordinary life, Wright made designs for three hundred commissions. One hundred thirty-five of them were built. These make up about a third of his professional output. Many of the designs were among his best. They were created at a time in life when most men would have been retired for twenty-five years. He seemed indestructible. Between 1950 and 1957, Wright flew to Europe six times, and each year he made the nomadic migrations between Taliesin North and Taliesin West.

Wright's design for the new Air Force Academy in Colorado could have been one of his finest creations. He seldom entered competitions, but he couldn't resist this possibility. All but two architectural studios had been eliminated: Wright and his much-despised Skidmore, Owings and Merrill. Suddenly Wright withdrew from the competition. The reason became clear in 1955 when *Architectural Forum* magazine revealed that the American Legion, an organization of veterans, had threatened to protest the selection of a pacifist and enemy sympathizer if he were selected. Rather than create a dark storm around the new academy, Wright had gracefully dropped out of the competition.

He won a battle in California when the liberal county of Marin asked him to design their Civic Center near the northern shore of San Francisco Bay. He was at the hearings before the board of supervisors to sign his contract when a document was introduced that supposedly detailed exactly how Wright had supported Communism and was a dangerous radical. Wright walked out. To their credit, the supervisors stopped the reading of the document, refusing to hear unsupported political slander against "a man of Mr. Wright's caliber." Wright returned shortly after touring the site again. He signed the contract. His comment to the attack on his reputation was, "I am what I am. If you don't like it, you can lump it." The Marin Civic Center was built to his design, his only municipal or government commission.

The center is not a great Wright design. A traveler along Route 101 crests a hill and the almost alien structure leaps out: it has an unexpected beauty, but it is more stage setting than architecture.

Like much of Wright's last work, the Civic Center doesn't express the basic function of architecture: to make logical connections between function, structure, and materials.

Art always has two sides that oppose each other: building up and tearing down. An artist looks at what he or she has created with a self-destructive, critical eye, saying, "This isn't good enough. I can do better than this." Great art doesn't flow onto the canvas or the drawing board in a continuous line. The best art is produced by this back-and-forth motion—hopeful creation, destructive criticism, revised hope, renewed criticism, and on and on. You can't be a great artist without being a severe critic of your own work. Perhaps this necessary self-destruction is why most artists are vulnerable to depression, the "worm's-eye view" that Wright mentioned many times throughout his life. But great artists—and Frank Lloyd Wright was one of them—also have a fund of self-worth that refills itself over and over. The masters of all the arts have that strange combination of self-destructive criticism and reviving optimism.

At the Fellowship he was revered too much. Olgivanna and the senior apprentices allowed no criticism. Life was comfortable. Who would question Wright's judgment? He was isolated from other architects and engineers who might argue with him and keep him sharp. He drifted into the dangerous success of believing in the fictitious Wright he had created for the public.

Age was fairly kind to the old fox. He lived well in his Taliesin princedom. His health was relatively fine, though he had nasty bouts with Ménière's Syndrome, which causes dizziness, nausea, and severe head pain. Wright was occasionally discovered crawling in his bedroom because he couldn't stand up without pitching over.

In the spring of 1959, Catherine, Wright's first wife, died quietly, one day short of her eighty-eighth birthday.

A month later Wright was taken to the hospital near Taliesin West in Phoenix for an intestinal obstruction and, unexpectedly, on the evening of April 9, 1959, died with no more than a sigh.

Wes Peters and one of "the boys" loaded the coffin into one of the Fellowship's nomadic trucks and drove nonstop to Taliesin North. The next day about forty friends, relatives, and neighbors followed a farm wagon bearing the coffin surrounded by flowers, drawn by two big horses, to the small cemetery a few hundred yards from Taliesin. He was buried with his mother, Anna Lloyd Wright, and Mamah Borthwick Cheney.

Olgivanna presided over the Taliesin Fellowship like a dragon over a tomb until she died in 1985. She left orders for the apprentices in her will. Without consulting Wright's children or relatives, they dug up Frank Lloyd Wright's body and cremated what remained. The ashes were mixed with Olgivanna's and built into one of Taliesin West's garden walls.

Many projects, including the Solomon R. Guggenheim Museum, were completed after his death.

Before Frank Lloyd Wright, most of American architecture had been copies of European and ancient Roman styles. Wright refused Europe's traditional models and created new, authentically American forms. Wright invented affordable, sensible, and livable architecture for common families. Today, his contributions go unnoticed because they have become part of our home language. We live Wright, in airy open-plan homes with bountiful light, a fluid connection with nature, centers of family warmth, natural materials. We search for Wright values in the homes we buy.

People and factors influenced him. Yet no one came before him to point the way. He invented a boldly different path and hacked it through customary building procedures, professional practice, severe criticism, two wars, and the FBI. His imagination was large and powerful. What he devised, others explored. He accused them of copying, but building on what works is progress. He was a natural giant of art and invention. There was never an architect who did as much for as long, or one who affected more people.

His work is found all over the country. People make Wright pilgrimages from one home to another; not just students of architecture, but folks who simply appreciate ingenuity and beauty. Our notions of what an architect is and what architecture is come from his flamboyant figure.

Frank Lloyd Wright's most brilliant and most colorful creation was Frank Lloyd Wright. He was not entirely truthful, not always pleasant, seldom easy, but he was an original character. The old fox was a dandy, wit, loudmouth, trickster, and the greatest con man we've ever had. He was also a disciplined engineer and a heavyweight creator whose heroic career went on for seventy-three productive years.

He was what he was. If we don't like it, we can lump it.

SOURCE NOTES

CHAPTER ONE
"adding tired to tired . . .": Gill, *Many Masks*, 48.

CHAPTER TWO
"Form ever follows function . . .": Sullivan, *Kindergarten Chats
and Other Writings*, 208.

CHAPTER THREE
"This will set American . . .": Secrest, *Frank Lloyd Wright*, 122.

CHAPTER FOUR
"Give me the luxuries . . .": Huxtable, *Frank Lloyd Wright*, 236.

CHAPTER FIVE
"without doodads . . .": Gill, *Many Masks*, 193.

CHAPTER SIX
"CRAMER SAYS WINDMILL . . . BUILD IT": Gill, *Many Masks*, 119.

CHAPTER SEVEN
"[Wright is] about 32 . . .": Secrest, *Frank Lloyd Wright*, 146.

"Can you not manage . . .": Gill, *Many Masks*, 141–42.

"If he is sane . . ." Gill, *Many Masks*, 159.

"A Home in a Prairie Town": *Ladies' Home Journal*, February 1901.

"good-time place": Gill, *Many Masks*, 175.

CHAPTER EIGHT

"a counting house": Gill, *Many Masks*, 184.

"the father feeling": Wright, *An Autobiography*, 113.

CHAPTER NINE

"marital slavery": Gill, *Many Masks*, 204.

CHAPTER TEN

"lord of my waking dreams": Secrest, *Frank Lloyd Wright*, 241.

CHAPTER ELEVEN

"shaking a design out . . .": Huxtable, *Frank Lloyd Wright*, 210.

"a monument to your genius": Gill, *Many Masks*, 264.

CHAPTER TWELVE

"I would rather have built . . .": Gill, *Many Masks*, 272.

"There are more leaking . . . cloud burst" and "That's how you know . . .": Gill, *Many Masks*, 271.

CHAPTER THIRTEEN

"machines for living": Secrest, *Frank Lloyd Wright*, 285.

"took souvenirs" and "For Sale: one romantic . . .": Secrest, *Frank Lloyd Wright*, 341.

"Montenegrin dancer": Huxtable, *Frank Lloyd Wright*, 170.

CHAPTER FOURTEEN

"automobile objective": Gill, *Many Masks*, 307.

"He was two hundred . . .": Secrest, *Frank Lloyd Wright*, 382.

"If the editor of this . . .": Secrest, *Frank Lloyd Wright*, 374.

"it would probably be . . .": Secrest, *Frank Lloyd Wright*, 462.

"Bury it!": Hoppen, *The Seven Ages*, 84.

"a democracy. When I'm . . .": Huxtable, *Frank Lloyd Wright*, 195.

"a house on the mesa": Gill, *Many Masks*, 35.

CHAPTER FIFTEEN

"Why, Stanley, you have . . .": Gill, *Many Masks*, 341.

"Whose fault is that? . . ." and "Dear Stanley: I didn't think . . .": Gill, *Many Masks*, 342.

"Come along, E. J.! . . .": Gill, *Many Masks*, 340.

CHAPTER SIXTEEN

"I never lost a cent . . .": Tafel, *Frank Lloyd Wright*, p. 168

CHAPTER SEVENTEEN

"vainglorious skyscraper": Secrest, *Frank Lloyd Wright*, 462.

"the mobocracy": Huxtable, *Frank Lloyd Wright*, 195.

CHAPTER EIGHTEEN

"the loveliest shelter . . .": Gill, *Many Masks*, 384.

"Well, this is what . . .": Gill, *Many Masks*, 372.

CHAPTER NINETEEN

"snake-oil salesman . . .": Gill, *Many Masks*, 357.

"Give them what . . .": Gill, *Many Masks*, 360.

"As a man does . . . :" Hoppen, *Seven Ages of Frank Lloyd Wright*, 87.

"Keep going!" and "Keep piling!": Gill, *Many Masks*, 364.

CHAPTER TWENTY-ONE

"undoubtedly the world's . . .": Secrest, *Frank Lloyd Wright*, 464.

"War solves nothing": Secrest, *Frank Lloyd Wright*, 485.

"gangsters": Secrest, *Frank Lloyd Wright*, 486.

"obsolete": Secrest, *Frank Lloyd Wright*, 485.

CHAPTER TWENTY-TWO

"Skidding, Owe-More and Sterile" and "the whiskey building looking . . .": Secrest, *Frank Lloyd Wright*, 548

"No great and good thing . . .": Gill, *Many Masks*, 438.

"Cousin Bob": Gill, *Many Masks*, 435.

CHAPTER TWENTY-THREE

"Sit down, Wes! . . .": Tafel, *Frank Lloyd Wright*, 158.

"a man of Mr. Wright's caliber" and "I am what I am . . .": Secrest, *Frank Lloyd Wright*, 544.

BIBLIOGRAPHY

Gill, Brendan. *Many Masks: A Biography of Frank Lloyd Wright.* New York: G. P. Putnam's Sons, 1987.

Hoppen, Donald W. *The Seven Ages of Frank Lloyd Wright: The Creative Process.* 1993. Reprint, New York: Dover Publications, 1998.

Huxtable, Ada Louise. *Frank Lloyd Wright.* Penguin Lives. New York: Viking, 2004.

Secrest, Meryle. *Frank Lloyd Wright.* New York: Knopf, 1992.

Sullivan, Louis I. *Kindergarten Chats and Other Writings* (1918). Reprint, New York: Dover Publications, 1979.

Tafel, Edgar (editor.) *Frank Lloyd Wright: Recollections by Those Who Knew Him.* Dover Publications, 2001.

Wright, Frank Lloyd. *An Autobiography.* Second Edition. New York: Duell, Sloan and Pearce, 1943.

Wright, Frank Lloyd. *Genius and the Mobocracy.* New York: Duell, Sloan and Pearce, 1949.

INDEX

NOTE: Page numbers in *italics* refer to illustrations.
FLW refers to Frank Lloyd Wright

PHOTO CREDITS